SONGS
of
GRACE

SONGS

of

GRACE

New Hymns for God and Neighbor

Carolyn Winfrey Gillette

DISCIPLESHIP RESOURCES

P O BOX 340003 • NASHVILLE, TN 37203-0003
www.discipleshipresources.org

Cover design by Paul Gant
Interior design by PerfecType, Nashville, TN

ISBN 978-0-88177-569-3

Library of Congress Control Number: 2009925605

For information regarding rights and permissions, contact Discipleship Resources, PO Box 340003, Nashville TN 37203-0003; fax 615-340-1789.

Discipleship Resources ® and design logos are trademarks owned by GBOD ®, Nashville, Tennessee. All rights reserved.

Contents

Worship

Church Celebrations

The Church in the World

Appendix

Indices

Preface

Hymns are prayers. There are so many different kinds of hymns because there are so many types of prayer. We offer God our praise and thankfulness, we confess our sin and ask for forgiveness, we cry out in lament, we wonder about God's world, we ask God for help, and we pray for our neighbors and the world. *Within these pages,* you will find all these kinds of prayers with one thing in common; they are prayers that speak of the grace of God working in our lives and in God's world, in joyful times as well as in difficult and challenging situations.

My work as a hymn writer comes from the glimpses of grace I have witnessed through my experiences in ministry. I have served as a pastor and a hospice chaplain. I have led mission trips and tutored inner city children, worked in the mountains of Kentucky and in the Philadelphia suburbs, listened to students in confirmation classes ask hard questions about the church, and visited elderly widows whose faith and trust in God left me in awe. I have organized volunteers for vacation Bible school and prayed with family members after the tragic death of their loved ones. At times I have asked God, "Why?" and at times I have felt God's presence more powerfully than I can describe. I have witnessed the terrifying and traumatic events of the last decade, and I have heard stories of love, hope and peace rising out of those events and many others. I have seen people in great need, and I have witnessed loving Christians reaching out to their neighbors in wonderful ways.

You have probably experienced a similar variety of joys, sorrows and challenges in your life, too. Often I write a hymn because of something I have seen or experienced, trusting that many other people have experienced something similar or have asked the same faith questions. Real life makes for wonderful hymn texts.

Karl Barth once said that preachers should preach with the Bible in one hand and the newspaper in the other. With the help of the Holy Spirit, the good news of scripture comes alive for us as we listen to the biblical story in the context of the world in which we live. Like sermons, hymns can help us to celebrate how faith and everyday life go together. The hymns in this book are a way for me to share the grace of God that I have witnessed;

they are intended to encourage the church (including myself) to respond to God's grace by loving our neighbors and reaching out to people in need.

After I wrote my first book of hymn texts, *Gifts of Love: New Hymns for Today's Worship* (Geneva Press, 2000), a number of people told me they were reading the hymns devotionally, as prayers, with their daily Bible reading. *Gifts of Love* ended up not only on the bookshelves of pastors and worship planners, it found its way to bedside tables with church members' daily devotional guides and well-thumbed Bibles.

With that in mind, I have changed the format for this second book of hymn texts. For each of these hymns, I have included a short note explaining something about the background of the hymn, my reason for writing it, and one or more biblical references. In addition, for each hymn, I have included a short meditation or reflection. This is meant to give more biblical or theological background on the hymn text, stories related to the hymn's content, and often, questions for reflection by the reader.

I hope that these hymns will continue to be sung and shared widely in worship; they are all written to common hymn tunes that are known and loved by many. Most of the tunes are old enough that they are no longer copyrighted and are in the public domain for anyone to use. The tunes are listed on the pages with the hymn texts and in an index at the end of the book. I hope that *Songs of Grace* will also end up on kitchen tables and bedside night stands, so that these words may be poetic, devotional reminders of God's grace. May these songs encourage you to love God and your neighbor, as my writing them has encouraged me in my own journey of faith and service.

Grace and Peace,
Carolyn Winfrey Gillette

Acknowledgements

I would like to thank many people who have helped and supported me in my hymn writing, encouraging me along the way:

Thank you to my husband and co-pastor Bruce, who has helped me in so many ways that I told him I would like to put his name on the cover of *Songs of Grace* right next to mine—but he humbly declined. Bruce has offered countless suggestions for hymn topics, lovingly critiqued my writing, put together indexes, answered thousands of emails related to my hymns from worship leaders around the world, and most of all, has been a friend who has shared the joy of sharing these hymns with others. I would not have written this book, or most of these hymns, without his loving encouragement.

Thank you to our children, John, Catherine and Sarah, who patiently and lovingly listened on many occasions to "Mom's latest hymn."

Thank you to my father-in-law, Gerald Gillette; thanks also to Tom and Nancy Stout, Freda A. Gardner, Tom Long, Debbie Harper, Charles Myers, Michael Morgan, Tom Hastings, and Arlo Duba for reviewing *Songs of Grace* and making many helpful suggestions.

Thank you to George Donigian, Nancy Bryan Crouch and Doug Hagler at Discipleship Resources for their gracious work in editing this book.

Thank you to all who have contacted us asking, "Have you ever written a hymn about . . ." and to those who have written to say that your church was encouraged in faith when they sang one of these hymns.

Thank you to people who have commissioned me to write new hymns for church anniversaries and ecumenical celebrations. Bob Kruschwitz, editor of Baylor University's *Christian Reflection* journal, has commissioned several hymns as well as the appendix article "Why We Sing" and I appreciate his willingness to have these all included in this book.

Thank you to those who have made my hymns available through their web site postings and links on the Internet: Jenee Woodard of *Text This Week*; Dean McIntyre of the Center for Worship Resourcing of the General Board of Discipleship of the United

Methodist Church (who also formatted twenty hymn texts with music), Roman Catholic Deacon Sil Galvin, Ronda Hughes of Church World Service, the Presbyterian Peacemaking Program, as well as the Presbyterian Hunger Program.

Thank you to the members of the First Presbyterian Church in Pitman, NJ, and the Limestone Presbyterian Church in Wilmington, DE, who have joyfully sung these words and encouraged me in my writing.

Most of all, thanks be to God from whom all blessings flow, who gave us the Word in Jesus Christ and who gives us words of praise and lament, joy and hope, love and grace to sing.

The Bible: Singing the Story

The Earth Is the Lord's

A number of churches have used this hymn when the lectionary has included the creation stories in Genesis 1 and 2 and Psalms 8 and 24. It has also been used for Earth Day worship services. This hymn was written when Bruce and I were serving as pastors in Pitman, New Jersey, which was one of the first EPA superfund clean-up sites in the United States because the LiPari Landfill had leaked into a creek miles from our community. We were very aware of life's interdependence and were thankful when it was cleaned up. This hymn text, formatted with the music, can be found on the United Methodist Church's Center for Worship Resourcing web site: <http://www.gbod.org>.

This book of hymns begins at the beginning, with songs celebrating God's creation, the first act of grace. Our faith begins with an understanding that everything belongs to God and that we are called to take care of all that God has made. The scriptures proclaim this theme again and again: "The earth is the Lord's and all that is in it" (Psalm 24:1). "And God said, 'Have dominion . . .'" (Genesis 1). "You have given them dominion over the works of your hands" (Psalm 8:6).

One summer morning, we woke up early to the sound of heavy machinery outside our window. We looked out and saw a crew of landscapers digging up a neighbor's yard. She had hired them to come in and completely re-do her lawn, plant new trees and shrubs, and prepare garden areas for flowers. They spent the next several days digging and planting. They listened to the owner's instructions and followed them, offering their own talents to make the yard as beautiful as it could be. It was not their yard to destroy or misuse. It was theirs to care for, for someone else—and they worked until it was beautiful.

In the same way, we are the gardeners in God's green earth. God commands us to have dominion over creation. Increasingly, people of faith are becoming aware that having dominion is not about ruling in an oppressive way, or taking advantage of the earth's resources and plundering them. Having dominion means caring for the earth, as a gardener cares for the land.

How do you celebrate God's creation? What steps are you taking to care for God's earth? Are there additional things you can do—maybe even things that will cost you in convenience or money? Have you (or has your church) ever considered installing solar paneling? Does your church have a program for reducing trash and promoting recycling? How energy-efficient is your form of transportation?

1. The Earth Is the Lord's

The earth is the Lord's and the fullness thereof.
Creation reminds us, O God, of your love.
By grace we are learning, as year leads to year,
We're called to be stewards, your caretakers here.

Your rainforests nurture the world that we share.
Your wetlands give animals shelter and care.
Your coral reefs cradle the life of the sea.
You've shown us, in love, what your good world can be.

Too often, O God, we abuse your good earth.
We fail to remember its beauty and worth.
We take from creation much more than we need,
We threaten your world through indifference and greed.

May we be good stewards of all that you give,
Protecting creation wherever we live.
May we be a church that renews and restores
And lovingly cares for this earth that is yours.

Tune: ST. DENIO 11.11.11.11 ("Immortal, Invisible, God Only Wise"), Welsh Folk Hymn, adapted in *Canaidau y Cyssegr*, 1839 Text: Copyright © 2001 by Carolyn Winfrey Gillette. All rights reserved.

On the Beach, the Waves of Waters

This hymn is a joyful celebration of God's creation at the seashore. It can be used at the beginning of summer when people are thinking of vacations, to encourage them to see God at work wherever they are. One church sang it on a vacation Bible school Sunday when the theme of the program was about the ocean. Psalms 104 and 148 celebrate the beauty of God's creation; they led me to wonder, "How might we sing God's praises as we enjoy God's gifts of creation at the beach?"

Recently our family spent several days at Bethany Beach in Delaware, where I wrote this hymn. Church friends Roy and Gena Timmer had made their beach home available to us, and those days were a real gift as we spent time together, away from the pressures of work.

It was delightful to write a hymn under a beach umbrella while watching children play paddle ball and teenagers enjoy the surf. There were children and adults who were getting into the spirit of sand castle competitions, and even people excitedly spotting dolphins far out in the water. The days were hot and sunny, and we enjoyed the crashing waves, warm sand, beautiful weather and people we love.

Psalm 104 includes these words: "Yonder is the sea, great and wide, creeping things innumerable are there, living things both small and great. There go the ships, and Leviathan that you formed to sport in it. These all look to you to give them their food in due season; when you give to them, they gather it up; when you open your hand, they are filled with good things" (Psalm 104:25-28). Another Psalm calls us to "Praise the Lord from the earth, you sea monsters and all deeps" (Psalm 148:7).

Vacations can be good times to reflect on the gifts of God's creation. Even if you stay at home on your vacation, and even if you are not able to be with the people you love and care about, look around and pay attention to what you see, hear and experience. How does creation sing God's story?

2. On the Beach, the Waves of Waters

On the beach, the waves of waters
Crash upon the sparkling sand.
Parents with their sons and daughters
Stroll and chatter, hand in hand.
Several people, watching, gazing,
Spot some dolphins swimming free.
God, your world is so amazing!
Thank you for the wondrous sea.

Later on, the storm clouds gather,
Rolling in upon the shore.
Lightning crashes, people scatter
As the rains begin to pour.
There is music in the thunder!
Soon the storms will pass on by.
God, we thank you for the wonder
Of the ever-changing sky.

In our homes and on vacation,
God, your love is every place.
You have made this good creation;
You have filled your world with grace.
Sea and land reflect your glory;
Beauty lights your sky above.
God, creation sings the story
Of your ever-constant love.

Tune: HYMN TO JOY 87.87 D ("Joyful, Joyful, We Adore Thee"), Ludwig van Beethoven, 1824
Alternate Tune: IN BABILONE 8.7.8.7.D (There's a Wideness in God's Mercy)

Creator, We Thank You for All You Have Made

This hymn was written as I was enjoying the beauty of the Shenandoah Valley in Virginia at the Massanetta Springs Bible Conference in August of 2006. It was first sung at the Union Presbyterian Church in Carneys Point, New Jersey, by a children's choir under the direction of Jim Green. The children took great joy in singing this song about finding the wonders of creation in things that are part of their lives. This is a hymn for people of all ages to sing, as we offer praise to God for the gifts of creation we see around us every day.

Psalm 95 proclaims, "For the Lord is a great God, and a great King above all gods. In his hand are the depths of the earth; the heights of the mountains are his also. The sea is his, for he made it, and the dry land, which his hands have formed" (Psalm 95:3-5). Psalm 104 also offers praise to God for the gifts of creation.

In cities, suburbs, and rural areas, too, we find evidence of God's creative, loving work. When we are praising and thanking God, it is good to look not just at the "big categories" of creation—land, sea and air—but to celebrate the little details. Take a walk down the street. Look for the weeds growing up through the cracks in the sidewalk. Can you identify one plant from another? Can you hear the differences in the birds' songs?

A recent report said that children today (and this may apply to many adults as well) are "nature deprived." Many of us in suburban and city settings go from climate-controlled homes to climate-controlled offices and schools, and then back home again. We spend our time with computer keyboards and video screens more than with "gardens in back corner lots" and "insects that hide out in old flower pots." When is the last time you sat in the grass and looked at cloud formations, or went out at night to see which phase the moon was in, and thanked God for the gifts that you saw?

3. Creator, We Thank You for All You Have Made

Creator, we thank you for all you have made:
For trees by the sidewalk that give us cool shade,
For grass-covered ball fields, for flowers downtown,
For wide autumn leaves that turn crispy and brown.

God, thank you for gardens on back corner-lots,
For insects that hide out in old flower pots,
For lions and polar bears living in zoos,
For high mountain trails that have beautiful views.

God, thank you for rainfall that ends a long drought,
For cracks in the sidewalk where little weeds sprout,
For birds that build nests in the tops of the trees,
For hot summer days when we feel a cool breeze.

O God, we give thanks for the places we go,
For cool mountain lakes and for trails in the snow,
For each city park and for each county fair,
For gifts of creation we see everywhere.

Tune: ST. DENIO 11 11.11 11 ("Immortal, Invisible, God Only Wise"), Welsh Folk Hymn, adapted in *Canaidau y Cyssegr*, 1839

Creator God, You Made the Earth

"Ancient Ways, New Hope" was the theme for the April 2002 conference of the National Association of Presbyterian Clergywomen (NAPC) in Albuquerque, NM. Marjorie J. Thompson, a Presbyterian Church(USA) minister who is the director of Pathways Center for Christian Spirituality with Upper Room Ministries and author of *Soul Feast: An Invitation to the Christian Spiritual Life* was the keynote speaker. I was asked by the NAPC to write a hymn based on the themes of Thompson's presentations on ancient wisdom and practices relating to the earth, to keeping Sabbath time, and to forgiveness and reconciliation. The tune, St. Columba, was named after an Irish missionary monk who introduced Christianity to parts of Scotland. Biblical texts for the hymn include Genesis 1-2:3, Romans 8:18-23, and Colossians 3:12-16.

So often in our lives, we tend to live day to day: we work, care for families, pay the bills, and try to cope with immediate needs and wants. Our Christian faith invites us to look at the big picture of what God has done and is doing through history. As we live each day, let us pause to thank God:

> for creation itself . . .
> for the goodness of all God has made . . .
> for putting creation into our care . . .
> for gifts of work-time and Sabbath-time . . .
> for healing and reconciliation in Jesus Christ . . .
> and for Christian communities where we share God's love and are sent out
>   to serve in Jesus' name.

Today, how have you celebrated God's creation as "a gift beyond comparing"? How have you acknowledged God's "pattern for creation" in your working and resting this week?

4. Creator God, You Made the Earth

Creator God, you made the earth,
A gift beyond comparing!
You called it good, you gave it worth,
You placed it in our caring.

You gave your gift of Sabbath rest,
Your pattern for creation.
You give us times to heal, to bless,
To join in celebration.

You give us Christ, who reconciled
The things of earth and heaven.
In him, you call each one your child!
What wondrous love you've given!

Because we've turned away from you,
This world still needs your healing.
Creation longs to be made new
Through Christ, your love revealing.

God, by your Spirit, may we be
Communities of caring,
That as we're healed, your world may see
The hope that we are sharing.

Tune: St. Columba 87.87 ("The King of Love My Shepherd Is"), Ancient Irish Melody
Alternate Tune: Dominus Regit Me

Our God, You Called to Moses

When Bill O'Connell was serving as pastor of the Glassboro Presbyterian Church in New Jersey, he led a presbytery worship service using a delightful chancel drama called, "Here I Am! Send Claude!" from David Steele's book *The Next Voice You Hear: Sermons We Preach Together* (Geneva Press, 1999). Bill asked me to write a hymn to go along with this chancel drama's theme of the call of Moses and our calling as Christians. This hymn was written to be a lighthearted complement to a lighthearted chancel drama, and yet it also has a thoughtful message. It could be used for services emphasizing God's call, including services of ordination and installation. The hymn is based on Exodus 3:1-4, 17 and 1 Corinthians 12.

Tony Campolo, an evangelist with a strong concern for social justice, recently told a group of pastors that mainline churches need to work harder at calling for commitment from their members. We need to challenge our children, youth and adults to serve God in the church and the world. All of us need to consider the gifts God has given us and find out how God is calling us to serve.

Sometimes, like Moses, we are hesitant. We may not have confidence in our own abilities. We may be concerned that we do not have time as family and work concerns press upon us. We may have been burned in the past; we may wonder how to discern God's call in our lives.

The Thoughtful Christian, a wonderful online resource for church discussion groups, has a session with the theme, "Listening to God's Call." The leader's guide suggests some ways God may call us:

> "Through a voice we hear in our heads, an idea or a 'vision,' especially one that refuses to go away; through words spoken to us by another person, especially a 'foreigner' from outside our accustomed world, or a stranger, or a traveler, or an opponent; through a sermon or other element of corporate worship; through reading the Bible; through a human need we become especially and intensely aware of; through a special talent we possess; through an event in daily life that speaks in some strong or unexpected way." (<www.thethoughtfulchristian.com>)

Once, when I attended church camp as a teenager, a seminary intern at the camp asked me, "Have you ever considered that God may be calling you to the ministry?" I had considered it, and that seminary student's comment helped me to consider God's call to ministry even more. Who has called you to do something for God? How might God be working through that person?

It has been said that where the needs of the world intersect with your own gifts and abilities and interests, there you will find God's call. What is God calling you to do? ❧

5. Our God, You Called to Moses

Our God, you called to Moses to set your people free.
What wrongly some suppose is: He answered easily.
"I'm not the one you're seeking!" he seemed instead to say.
"My strength is not in speaking; God, find another way!"

And yet, O Lord, you told him to trust in what you said.
Your strength would surely hold him through every day ahead.
Though many would oppose him, by your own name he'd know:
You were the one who chose him to help your people go.

You call each congregation to serve the lost and poor.
We doubt our own vocation; we ask, "Lord, are you sure?"
Yet you give gifts for sharing, you show us what to say.
Your Spirit gives us daring to serve Christ every day.

Tune: LLANGLOFFAN 76.76 D ("Rejoice, Rejoice, Believers"), Welsh Folk Melody
Text: Copyright © 2000 by Carolyn Winfrey Gillette. All rights reserved.

Why Is This Night Different?

Many congregations have found that it can be meaningful to celebrate the Jewish origins of the Lord's Supper with a Passover Seder on Maundy Thursday. This hymn, written for use on Maundy Thursday, lifts up some of the traditional elements of the Jewish celebration of the Passover Seder. The final verse recognizes the uniquely Christian adaptation of it and can be sung separately, after the Lord's Supper is shared. Exodus 5:12-15 tells about the suffering of God's people and Exodus 12–13 tells about the Jewish celebration; the gospel stories in Matthew 26:26-30; Mark 14:22-25; Luke 22:14-23 tell us about the Passover meal, the Last Supper, that Jesus shared with his disciples.

Luke tells us, "Then came the day of Unleavened Bread, on which the Passover lamb had to be sacrificed. So Jesus sent Peter and John, saying, 'Go and prepare the Passover meal for us that we may eat it'" (Luke 22:7-8). It was at that meal with his disciples that Jesus said, "This is my body . . ."

Did you ever share in a Seder? What do you remember most about it? The story of the Exodus of God's people from Egypt is not meant to be a story that remains in the past tense. It is more than ancient history. We pray, "God, help us to know that it's our story, too!" How have you known captivity in body, mind, or spirit? How has God given you the gift of freedom in your life? How have you known the "sweetness of hope ever-savored," and "the promise that God saves"? How has God's gift of salvation encouraged you to serve others who are captive to oppression, poverty, sin and death?

6. Why Is This Night Different?

"Why is this night different from all of the others?"
This night we remember how God set us free.
This night we remember our fathers and mothers
Whom God reached out to save from harsh slavery.

We eat bitter herbs to recall how they suffered;
The salt water tells of their tears and their cries.
The lamb is the sacrifice each household offered;
The matzo is the bread with no time to rise.

Haroseth reminds how the people long labored
In making the mortar; what weary, worn slaves!
And yet in its sweetness is hope ever-savored,
And in each cup of wine, the promise: God saves!

Through symbols we share here, your story is spoken;
God, help us to know that it's our story, too!
For as we are saved we are sent to the broken,
Till all know peace and joy, till all are made new.

****

[After the Lord's Supper is shared]

Lord Jesus, you joined in the great celebration,
Then gave us a new meal to joyfully share.
You blessed bread and wine and you offered salvation;
Now send us out to serve, Lord, this is our prayer!

Tune: KREMSER 12 11.12 11 ("We Gather Together"), *Nederlandtsch Gedenckclanck*, 1626
Text: Copyright © 2000 by Carolyn Winfrey Gillette. All rights reserved.

O God, Be Merciful to Me

This hymn was requested by friends in Australia. One of the joys of the Internet is hearing from friends literally around the world who have contacted me about the hymns I have written. This couple in Perth, John and Val Fizzell, traded emails with us and made suggestions for hymns at various times, including this one. I am always open to hearing suggestions for topics of new hymns.

Psalm 51 is in the lectionary for every Ash Wednesday. This hymn could also be used as a prayer of confession, sung or read, on any Sunday. The hymn, formatted with music, may be found online at <www.gbod.org/worship>, the website of the Center for Worship Resourcing of the United Methodist Church.

One Sunday, a church member came up to me after the worship service and said, "I've always wondered why we say a prayer of confession and hear an assurance of forgiveness *every single week,* but today I understand. Today, it jumped out at me just what this means! Even though I've really messed up in my life, God forgives me! That's really a powerful thing, isn't it?"

Every Sunday, our worship service includes a prayer of confession. After an opening hymn of praise and adoration in which we sing about how wonderful and holy God is, the prayer of confession is a way of putting things in perspective. We acknowledge the ways we have fallen short of following God's way. The prayer is followed by words of great comfort and joy, as we hear an assurance of God's forgiving love from the words of scripture.

Psalm 51 is a wonderful prayer of confession that has been used by people of faith for many centuries. Find a Bible and read this Psalm one time straight through, and then go back and read it again. Which one line speaks to you today? Pray that one line again. Meditate on its words. Now go back and pray the entire Psalm again. How does God speak through this Psalm to you?

7. O God, Be Merciful to Me

O God, be merciful to me
Because your love is strong;
Now wash me from iniquity
And cleanse me from all wrong.

These words are old, but still they live
Within our hearts today.
We cry to you: "O God, forgive!"
And "Wash our sins away!"

My sin has kept me far from you;
Your wrath is justified.
Why is it, Lord? The things I do
Have crushed my bones inside!

I try to make it on my own
As if I'm all I need,
Until I find I'm all alone,
Wrapped up in pride and greed.

Yet this is not the final word,
For you forgive our sin!
When we return to you, O Lord,
You give us joy again.

Tune: CRIMOND CM ("The Lord's My Shepherd, I'll Not Want'), Jessie Seymour Irvine, 1872.
Alternate Tune: ST. ANNE, ("Our God, Our Help in Ages Past")

An Eagle Is Soaring

This text turns and dives with the tune to which it is sung. The words are a reference to Isaiah 40:30-31.

Did you ever watch an eagle in flight? It moves so gracefully as it glides through the air with its wings outstretched. I remember hearing in a lecture how an eagle puts forth very little effort as it soars because it takes advantage of the updrafts of air. It rides the waves of air upward and then gently glides down toward earth, until it catches the next updraft.

Isaiah 40:30-31 reminds us, "Even youths will faint and be weary, and the young will fall exhausted; but those who wait for the Lord shall renew their strength, they shall mount up with wings like eagles, they shall run and not be weary, they shall walk and not faint." Sometimes we struggle so hard to please God and to try to sustain our faith on our own. We flap our spiritual wings, trying to take off on our own, convinced that we can succeed in faith and life if only we try hard enough.

Instead, we are called to remember God's grace. God is waiting to lift us up and renew us, if only we will wait for the Lord and be open to receiving God's love and strength. How do you need to wait and listen to God today?

8. An Eagle Is Soaring

An eagle is soaring and turning and diving;
It stretches its wings to the currents of air.
It gracefully moves without effort or striving;
The updrafts will carry its flight anywhere.
How hard, Lord, we struggle and work for your blessing;
May we see your grace in the eagle above.
For you will renew us when we wait and listen,
And you will uphold us in strength and in love.

Tune: ASH GROVE 6 6 11.6 6 11 D, Welsh folk melody
Text: Copyright © 2006 by Carolyn Winfrey Gillette. All rights reserved.

We Love to Sound Your Praises

This hymn was inspired by a Bible study on Jeremiah by **the Rev. Dr. Richard Boyce**, the Associate Professor of Preaching and Pastoral Leadership at Union Theological Seminary and Presbyterian School of Christian Education at Charlotte, during the 2007 Massanetta Springs Bible Conference in western Virginia. Biblical references include: Jeremiah 2:5,11,13; 4:19; 8:18; John 3:16, Romans 5:8-10, Philippians 4:4 and Revelation 19.

Jeremiah is sometimes called the "crying prophet." He saw how God's people were turning away from God, and he said again and again that God's heart was breaking. Jeremiah quoted God as saying, "What wrong did your ancestors find in me that they went far from me, and went after worthless things and became worthless themselves?" (Jeremiah 2:5). What are the problems in our own society and world that cause God to weep?

Jeremiah goes on to say: "My people have . . . forsaken me, the fountain of living water, and dug out cisterns for themselves, cracked cisterns that can hold no water" (2.13). Who would be foolish enough to turn down a source of good, clean water, and drink only from polluted, broken cisterns made by human hands? No one, we are quick to say. Yet, how much time do we spend reading the Bible compared to the amount of time we spend mindlessly surfing the Internet or watching television? How much time do we spend in worship, compared to the time we spend shopping? How much time do we spend seeking spiritual growth, and how much into seeking financial gain? Do we choose living water, or water from broken wells?

The good news is that God offers us the fullness of life in Jesus Christ. We are forgiven people! We work and wait for the day when laments will no longer be sung or heard, and when all God's creation will be singing alleluias. ❧

9. We Love to Sound Your Praises

We love to sound your praises, To lift our hands above,
To sing how grace amazes, To celebrate your love.
Yet, God, your world is grieving; Is your heart breaking, too?
May we cry out, believing Laments can honor you.

Like Jeremiah, crying For cities that were lost,
We see the children dying Who know war's awful cost.
Each day repeats the story; Sin takes its toll again.
How can we sing your glory When our hearts break with them?

The scope of sin is broader Than what the late news tells;
Rejecting living water, We dig our broken wells.
In gods of our own making We look for joy each day;
O God, is your heart breaking When we all turn away?

O God, you came to save us In Christ, your suffering Son.
In his death you forgave us; In his life, joy is won!
And when this world is suffering, When songs of grief abound,
May we work for your kingdom, Till alleluias sound!

Tune: Passion Chorale 76.76 D ("O Sacred Head, Now Wounded"), Hans Leo Hassler, 1601.
Text: Copyright © 2007 by Carolyn Winfrey Gillette. All rights reserved.

Remember Me

This hymn lifts up some of the major stories of the Bible in which God calls us into a covenant relationship. The hymn mentions the stories of the Exodus, Jesus sharing his last meal with his disciples, and the risen Christ appearing to the disciples and to the early church. Biblical references related to the theme of this hymn include: Exodus 20:1-2; Deuteronomy 6:4-9; 1 Corinthians 11:23-25; Matthew 26:26-29; Mark 14:22-25; Luke 22:14-19; 24:13-32; Hebrews 13:8; John 14:26, 17:18; Matthew 28:18-20; Acts 1:8.

In John 14:26, we have Jesus' promise: "The Advocate, the Holy Spirit, whom the Father will send in my name, will teach you everything, and remind you of all I have said to you." Living the Christian faith is an act of forever remembering who God is and whose we are. We live out our faith in gratitude for God's saving love as told in the Old and New Testaments. Someone recently asked me the often-repeated question: "Why do I need to be part of a church? Why can't I just be a Christian off by myself somewhere?" One of the joys of being part of the community of God's people is that we share a common story and a common memory of God's love. We tell each other the story and then we share the story with this world that desperately needs to hear it.

There are times when any one of us may not remember and treasure this story on our own. I may be distracted by work. You may be overwhelmed by family responsibilities and challenges. Another person may be seduced by this culture that encourages us to forget God's love. Still another may suffer the kind of memory loss that comes with Alzheimer's disease or another form of dementia. Yet, as a community, we gather for worship and we remember—together. We live out the story of what God has done for us and what God continues to do—together. We celebrate God's love together, and we are thankful. ❦

10. Remember Me

Remember me—the God who saves—
For back in Egypt you were slaves;
Then by my hand I set you free.
Now keep my law. Remember me.

Remember me in bread and wine
Whene'er you share this meal of mine.
I gave my life to set you free.
With thanks and praise, remember me.

Remember me in all you do,
For I'm alive! I walk with you.
I was, I am, and I shall be.
O church I love, remember me.

Our God, we hear! We're called and freed!
Your Spirit gives us memory.
Now send us out that we may share
Your love's great story everywhere.

Tune: O WALY WALY LM ("Though I May Speak"), English folk melody.
Text: Copyright © 2001 by Carolyn Winfrey Gillette. All rights reserved.

"Fear Not!" the Angel Said

Many churches prefer to use traditional Christmas carols at Christmas, yet there are creative ways to introduce new songs related to Jesus' birth. The Sunday after Christmas, family programs and hymn-sings are all times and places where a new hymn might be used to offer different insights related to the Christmas story. See: Luke 2:1-20; 2 Corinthians 8:9; John 6:35.

There is so much fear in our world today. The newspapers and TV news shows are full of stories of wars between nations, and violence in our neighborhoods. Throughout my years as a pastor, I have had occasions to listen to the concerns and fears of church members and others as they have struggled to comprehend how violence has affected their families, communities and world. Some older members have told me that they wish the world could "go back to the way it was"—before 9/11 and the war that has followed, or when they felt comfortable walking in their neighborhoods, or when schools were safer for children. Those people were expressing their longing for peace, wholeness and freedom from fear. Fear too often leads to violence. We are taught that the way to respond to our insecurities—as nations, communities, or individuals—is to lash out at others, before they have a chance to hurt us.

When Jesus was born, the message of the angel to the shepherds was "Fear not!" "Don't be afraid!" (Luke 2:1-20). The angel's words were ones of comfort to the shepherds struggling to make a living, and they are words of comfort to the hungry child, the homeless refugee, the battered woman, and all those who are open to receiving them today. God's grace is greater than anything this world can throw at us. Further, when the church responds with compassion and care, we bring God's hope to places where there has been fear.

This same message, "Fear not," is also needed by people whose lives appear comfortable, but who have lost their sense of connection to God. We all need the Bread of Life to satisfy our deepest spiritual hunger for God (John 6:35).

The church desperately needs this message, too. Sometimes we let fear and pride divide us—one denomination from the next, and one group of believers from another. The love of God in Jesus Christ can overcome all the things that divide us, and God can overcome all the things that make us afraid.

What do you fear? How are the words "Fear not!" good news for you?

11. "Fear Not!" the Angel Said

"Fear not!" the angel said, "God's joy is in the air!
Now go to Bethlehem and see a newborn baby there.
A Savior, yet a child! So young, and yet the Lord!"
God's grace astounds, God's love surrounds this sinful, hurting world.

Fear not, you hungry child, you homeless refugee,
You battered woman, burdened down—God came to set you free.
For God's own Son was poor; He cried and suffered, too.
God's grace astounds; God's love abounds for people just like you.

Fear not when questions come: "How can I know God's way?"
"Do my possessions weigh me down?" "Can God change me today?"
For Jesus came to be true bread that satisfies;
And in his birth, God touched the earth; Christ saves, forgives, and guides.

Fear not, you church of Christ, distracted and distressed,
For long ago in troubled times, Christ came, and we were blest.
Our Prince of Peace is born—our light, our life, our song!
In him we see our unity; in him God makes us strong.

Tune: TERRA BEATA SMD ("This is My Father's World"), Traditional English melody; adapt. by
Franklin L. Sheppard, 1915

Down by the Jordan

Near the beginning of each one of the first three gospels, there is the story of Jesus' baptism. Jesus was baptized not because of any sinfulness on his part, but to "fulfill all righteousness." In other words, God said it was the right thing for Jesus to do. As one who shared the human condition, Jesus went to be baptized, too. This hymn may be used on the Sunday celebrating the Baptism of the Lord, or when a baptism is celebrated. Biblical references include Matthew 3:1-17; Mark 1:1-11; Luke 3:1-22 and John 1:6-8, 14-34

Our daughter Catherine recently got her license, and she is a good and careful driver. With a new driver in the family, though, we see traffic patterns through new eyes. We have noticed how many divided highways there are, and how many times it is absolutely necessary to do U-turns to get to a store or business on the left-hand side of the road. It simply doesn't accomplish anything to keep on driving straight ahead.

John the Baptist was a fiery preacher who called people to turn their lives around. John made it clear: everything good in life starts with God's forgiveness. People are called to respond to what God has done by making those U-turns, by turning our lives around. In faith as in traffic, U-turns can be scary, but they are often necessary to get where we need to go.

Are there any areas of life where you can see you're getting nowhere, and the only thing to do is to say a prayer and turn around, getting back on the right track? How can we respond to God who graciously says to us in baptism, "You are mine"?

Both of the last two verses of this hymn end with words that acknowledge the connection between baptism and vocation. "Your work began in those waters." "Let's take the good news and share it." Jesus' ministry began with his baptism. When we are baptized, we begin our ministry.

One of the ways we recognize this connection in our congregation is through a special offering in honor of the child who has been baptized. As the worship service ends on a baptism Sunday, two children stand at the doors of the sanctuary with woven baskets from Kenya to receive a special "second offering." The money is sent to a school in Kenya for children who have been orphaned by AIDS and by the war in the Sudan. And so, the baptized child's ministry begins, as money is raised in his or her name to help other children in God's world.

12. Down by the Jordan

Down by the Jordan, a prophet named John was baptizing,
Preaching a message the people found bold and surprising:
"God will forgive! Show that you'll change how you live!
Surely God's new day is rising!"

There by the river, the crowd came with great expectation:
"Are you God's Chosen One, sent here to rescue our nation?"
"No!" John replied. "He who is mightier than I
Judges and offers salvation."

Jesus, you went to be baptized with all of the others,
Taking your place among sinners, God's lost sons and daughters.
Then with great love, God's Spirit came as a dove!
Your work began in those waters.

Here in the Church, we are baptized and filled with God's Spirit.
Freed and forgiven, we're welcomed with joy! Can you hear it?
This is God's sign! This is how God says, "You're mine!"
Let's take the good news and share it!

Tune: LOBE DEN HERREN 14 14.478 ("Praise Ye the Lord, the Almighty"), *Stralsund Erneuerten Gesangbuch*, 1665.

Text: Copyright © 2000 by Carolyn Winfrey Gillette. All rights reserved.

Our Lord, You Were Sent

This hymn deals with the gospel lesson for the first Sunday in Lent every year—the story of Jesus' temptation. Matthew and Luke tell us about the three temptations faced by Jesus, though they change the order a bit; this hymn uses the order found in Matthew. Henri Nouwen's writings on Jesus' temptation (found originally in *Sojourners* magazine and later in a book titled *The Selfless Way of Christ*), Parker Palmer's book *The Active Life*, and Wayne Oates' book *Temptation* were all helpful to me as I wrote this hymn. The stories of Jesus' baptism can be found in Matthew 4:1-11; Mark 1:12-13; and Luke 4:1-13. Hebrews 2:18 and 4:15 give us further insights on Jesus' temptation.

Look carefully at the temptations of Jesus. In each one of them, Jesus was tempted to believe that something was excusable when it was really very wrong. He was tempted to let things slide, to do what seemed easiest at the time, to say that "the means justified the ends."

"How could it be wrong?" we often wonder. If we just bend the rules a little here, if we just close our eyes to something there, if we just do what is most convenient, or if we simply do what benefits us, surely God will understand. How could it be wrong?

Jesus answered each of these temptations by quoting the scriptures. He said, "It is written . . ." Those who read the Bible prayerfully every day and who study its meaning have a wonderful tool of faith that helps in ethical decision-making. This doesn't mean that they can necessarily quote a specific Bible verse for each situation, yet they do know the major themes of the Old and New Testaments. Their minds and hearts are filled with Bible stories that speak of love and justice, peace and compassion, forgiveness, generosity, and seeking God's kingdom first. They know the Psalms that strengthen them and the passages that encourage them through tough times.

All people use tools in one way or another. How is the Bible a tool that helps you make decisions as a disciple of Jesus Christ? Are there any passages of scripture that you have memorized that help you in times of trouble? ❧

13. Our Lord, You Were Sent

Our Lord, you were sent to a place wild and vast
To ponder your mission, to pray and to fast;
Then hungry and weary, you faced night and day
The subtle temptations to turn from God's way.

How could it be wrong to want bread on the shelf?
To seek, in one's serving, to first serve one's self?
But by God's own word you remained ever sure:
It's only in God that our lives are secure.

How could it be wrong to step out and to dare,
To prove with great drama the depths of God's care?
But you knew God's word, true since all time began:
It's wrong to expect God to work by our plan.

How could it be wrong to just once bow the knee,
To shake hands with sin to achieve victory?
Yet you made it clear that no matter the cost:
Your path was obedience, your way was the cross.

Our Lord, in your struggle you chose to obey;
God's word filled your heart and you trusted God's way.
Now risen, you save us from sins that destroy;
You give us your Spirit, your peace and your joy.

Tune: FOUNDATION 11 11.11 11 ("How Firm a Foundation"), American Folk Melody, Funk's *Genuine Church Music*, 1832

Jesus, You Once Called Disciples

This hymn was originally published in *The Presbyterian Outlook* magazine. The lists of disciples found in the gospels are slightly different from each other. This hymn begins with the listing of twelve disciples which is found in Matthew 10:1-4. The four gospels together give a complete picture of Jesus calling not only the twelve, but also women (including Mary, Martha and the woman at the well), other men, and children.

The line "some are brought up in your way" is a reference to 2 Timothy 1:5 where Timothy is described as one raised in the faith by his grandmother Lois and mother Eunice. These women passed on the faith to their family, so that for Timothy, faith was something he grew into over a period of time.

Biblical references include: Matthew 4:18-22, 10:1-41, Luke 10:38-42, John 11:17-27, Luke 8:1-3, John 4:1-42, John 6:9, 19:25- 27, Acts 9:1-22, and 2 Timothy 1:5.

When I was growing up, I went to church camp every summer; camp offered many experiences that helped me to grow in my faith. One summer, though, I had a counselor who was particularly trying. He was convinced that for a person to be truly saved, he or she had to have a miserable past, a dramatic lightning-bolt encounter with God, and a salvation date to write on the calendar. Yet my experience was something completely different. I knew, in the words of an old gospel hymn, that "my Redeemer lives; he lives within my heart."

I knew the joy of having been born into a loving, Christian family. Some of my earliest memories are of standing on the pew between my parents during worship, trying to sing the hymns. My family shared devotions every day; as a teenager, I remember hearing nightly readings from the books of E. Stanley Jones, a Methodist missionary and evangelist. I loved youth group and Church school and worship. Sometimes as a little child I had trouble sitting still during the sermon—as many children do—but I knew the joy of God's gift of salvation from the time I was very young. Many people come to faith as Paul did, in a dramatic way, but I can relate to Timothy, whose family nurtured him in faith.

How did you come to be a disciple of Jesus? Did you come to faith in a dramatic way or were you nurtured in the faith from the time you were an infant? Sit down with a Bible and a notepad and make a list of Bible stories that show the wonderful variety of ways that God calls different people. Which one can you relate to the most?

14. Jesus, You Once Called Disciples

Jesus, you once called disciples, choosing twelve to follow you:
Simon (also known as Peter), Andrew and Bartholomew,
Philip, Thomas, James, and Matthew, Simon, Thaddaeus, John, and James—
Then there was the one called Judas. These were your disciples' names.

Women, too, were your disciples, sitting, learning, at your feet.
Mary knew your word was precious, even more than food to eat.
Martha trusted in your power when her brother Laz'rus died.
Women shared your journey, Lord, and stayed when you were crucified.

Lord, so many heard and followed, like the woman at the well.
Meeting you, the living water, she sought others she could tell.
Like the boy with loaves and fishes, like Zacchaeus in the tree,
Many gladly heard your message; many shared your ministry.

Jesus, still you call your people, "Come and follow me today!"
Some, like Paul, feel sudden wonder; some are brought up in your way.
Lord, no matter how we meet you, by your Spirit, make us new.
May we know your living presence; may we daily follow you.

Tune: IN BABILONE 87.87 D ("There's a Wideness in God's Mercy"), Dutch Melody arranged by Julius Roentgen (1855-1933)

O Lord, You Called Disciples

This hymn was originally written for the 100th anniversary celebration (August 11, 2002) of the First Presbyterian Church in Bay Minette, Alabama. Scripture references include Matthew 4:18-22, Mark 1:16-20, Luke 5:1-11, John 1:35-51; John 4:1-45, Luke 8:1-3, and Matthew 25:31-46.

Jesus had many more than twelve disciples, and this hymn, like the previous one, recognizes the faith of many people who sought to follow him. One of these was the woman at the well, and amazingly, John's gospel tells us the story of her conversation with Jesus in great detail. When she realized that Jesus had spoken God's truth to her, she went back and told her friends and neighbors. She invited them to come and meet Jesus, too.

Churches grow when people are inviting. Today, I was putting up vacation Bible school fliers around town when a mother and her two children got out of their car at a shopping center. The girl said hello, and the mother began talking with me as well. I mentioned that our church was getting ready for VBS and said that we would love to have them join us. The conversation was a quick and informal one—nothing profound. But who knows? Maybe God will use it today . . . or tomorrow . . . or in a year. Maybe they will remember that someone from a church said to them, "We'd love for you to join us. Come and see what's happening at our church."

"Come and see" is an even more effective invitation when it is spoken to people we know. Studies have shown that the majority of people who are invited to church by family or friends will actually come and visit. How can you invite someone to "come and see" the good news of Jesus Christ that your church has to offer?

15. O Lord, You Called Disciples

O Lord, you called disciples, proclaiming, "Come and see!"
And so an invitation began your ministry.
Then Andrew called his brother, and Peter came to you;
More men and women followed, and little children, too.

You met a busy woman out in the noon-day sun.
You shared God's love, you listened; you told all she had done.
She called her friends and neighbors and brought them face to face
With you, the living water, the bearer of God's grace.

O Christ, your invitation has reached from year to year!
Through some who heard you calling, a church was founded here.
As faithful people served you a century ago,*
They soon invited others; your church began to grow.

God, by your Holy Spirit, now send us in your name
To serve the lost and outcast, the poor for whom you came.
Through gifts of hope and healing, through loving ministry,
May we reach out, inviting the world to "Come and see!"

*Or "as faithful people served you so many years ago,"

Tune: LANCASHIRE 76.76 D ("The Day of Resurrection!"), Henry Thomas Smart, 1835.
Text: Copyright © 2002 by Carolyn Winfrey Gillette. All rights reserved.

She Came to Jesus

"She came to Jesus" was written for the celebration of the 35th anniversary of the ordination of the Rev. Dr. Dorothea Brooks. The hymn is based on the sermon text for that worship service, Matthew 15:21-28. See also Mark 7:24-30.

When the Canaanite woman first approached Jesus asking for help, "he did not answer her at all." When he did answer, he said, "I was sent only to the lost sheep of the house of Israel" (Matthew 15:23-24). Many people are perplexed by Jesus' initial response to this desperate mother. Why did he speak to her in the way that he did?

While his words seem harsh at first, he did have a conversation with her about her faith, and he did listen to what she had to say. Then he healed her child. He confirmed what she believed—that God's love is "not bounded by place," or culture, or anything else.

So many people whose lives were touched by Jesus were outsiders; they were people "outside the fold." Why are we sometimes hesitant to reach out in ministry to other people? Do you know anyone who—following Jesus' example—has a wonderful gift for breaking down the stubborn barriers between people from different backgrounds and cultures? ❧

16. She Came to Jesus

She came to Jesus from outside the fold—
Canaanite woman! Persistent and bold!
Looking to Jesus, she wanted to see
One who would help her and set her child free.

Claiming a blessing, a touch of God's grace,
She knew God's love was not bounded by place.
Jesus, you listened, debated—then healed—
For in her asking, her faith was revealed.

God, you still bless those who seek you in prayer.
You welcome dreamers who faithfully dare.
In Christ, now risen, your mercy extends:
Those on the outside are welcomed as friends.

Bless by your Spirit this minister here
Who has served faithfully year after year—
Breaking down barriers, persistent and bold,
Leading your people back into your fold.

Tune: SLANE 10 10.9 10 ("Be Thou My Vision"), Irish Ballad.
Text: Copyright © 2002 by Carolyn Winfrey Gillette. All rights reserved.

O God of Light, May Our Light Shine

The World Day of Prayer 2005 had the theme "Let our Light Shine." This hymn, "O God of Light, May Our Light Shine," was written for the ecumenical celebration of the World Day of Prayer hosted by the Hockessin United Methodist Church in Delaware. See Matthew 5:13-16, Psalm 27:1 and Psalm 119:105.

When have you had an experience of being in complete darkness? When have you experienced just a little bit of light in the midst of shadowed darkness? When I was about six years old, we lived for a summer with my grandparents in a town in West Virginia. I remember lying down to go to sleep in an upstairs bedroom, in that dark house with its shuttered windows. When my parents went downstairs after tucking me in, they seemed to be miles away, at the bottom of an ancient, creaking, enclosed staircase, then around the corner and down the hall in the living room. I would lie awake with the covers pulled up past my chin, waiting in the darkness for cars to pass by on the road outside. Every time a car went by, its headlights made a wonderful pattern of light. The light would shine through the shuttered windows and then move across the walls and ceiling of that dark bedroom. I loved every little bit of light that came in that room.

Jesus said, "You are the light of the world . . . Let your light shine before others" (Matthew 5:14, 16). We are called to be God's light for others. Light can be a comforting presence. It can offer peace and security. It can guide the way for those who are searching. The light we offer is not our own, but the light of Jesus Christ working in and through us. And "when our own faith is flickering out," we trust Jesus who said, "I am the light of the world" (John 8:12). ❦

17. O God of Light, May Our Light Shine

O God of light, may our light shine
In ways that serve and honor you.
May we be loving, just and kind,
Proclaiming Christ in all we do.

God, where your people are oppressed
And where they cry out in despair,
Make us your light—to heal, to bless—
A witness, Lord, that you are there.

Christ, when your way is pushed aside
By those who trust in wealth and might,
Make us your lamps that we may guide
A searching world to your love's light.

O Spirit, in this world of doubt,
We often sin and drift away.
When our own faith is flickering out,
Shine on our path and light our way.

Tune: CANONBURY LM ("Lord, Speak to Me, That I May Speak"), Adapt. from Robert Schumann, 1839.

Alternate Tune: O WALY WALY

Text: Copyright © 2005 by Carolyn Winfrey Gillette. All rights reserved.

Bigger Barns

This hymn is based on the Parable of the Rich Fool found in Luke 12:13-21. It also looks at the disparity between rich and poor found in Luke 16:19-31, the Rich Man and Lazarus: "Can our bigger barns be good when poor neighbors know despair?"

"More" is a central word in our language and culture. We grow up wanting more toys, more electronic gadgets, more possessions, more money—and we hope that these things will give us more security and more happiness. Jesus told this parable about a man who spent his life collecting more and more possessions, until he needed bigger storage areas for all the things he owned. This is just one of many times that Jesus talked about wealth and possessions. He made it clear that we cannot serve two masters—God and money. If we serve our possessions, we will find in the end (literally, at the end of our lives) that we have nothing permanent. If we serve God, we will have all the richness of God's presence in our lives.

On the plane home from a mission trip to Honduras, I asked mission team members to write down some things they had learned. Many of the responses had a common theme: "I learned that I have too much stuff." "I learned that people can be happy with very few possessions." "I found out that my faith in God matters more than what we own." "I learned that my possessions can distract me from the things that really matter, like my relationship with God." "I learned that I shouldn't put my security in the things I own."

When we try to keep things for ourselves, we may end up losing them. If we spend money on an unending stream of possessions, we may regret it later on. If we invest in the stock market, our investments may decline in value. If we try to store up possessions, they may be destroyed. But money that we give to help people in need builds something precious that can never be taken away. The value of a gift given in love is eternal. It will bless others and us, too.

What can you do today to put your security where it belongs—in God, and not in your possessions?

18. Bigger Barns

"Bigger barns are what I need," so a rich man said one day.
"From my worries I'll be free when my wealth is stored away."
"Fool!" God said, "Today you'll die!" Will that wealth mean anything?
All life's blessings really lie in the gifts that wealth can't bring.

"Bigger barns are what we need for our money, gadgets, more!"
Lord, we're tempted to believe having wealth, we'll be secure!
Somewhere children cry for food or to have a doctor's care.
Can our bigger barns be good when poor neighbors know despair?

God of love, we long to know what will make us truly blest.
Jesus taught us long ago wealth won't give us peace or rest.
You are our security! Safe in you, we serve, O Lord.
May we find we're rich indeed when we're sharing with the poor.

Tune: ABERYSTWYTH 77.77 D ("Jesus, Lover of My Soul"), Joseph Parry, 1879.
Text: Copyright © 2001 by Carolyn Winfrey Gillette. All rights reserved.

Who Is My Neighbor?

Jesus was asked, "What must I do to inherit eternal life?" He told the man who asked him, "Love the Lord your God . . . and love your neighbor as yourself" (Luke 10:25ff). Then the man asked the obvious question, "Who is my neighbor?" This hymn is based on the parable Jesus tells to answer that question. See also Romans 13:9-10, Galatians 5:14, James 2:8 and 1 John 4:20-21.

The story of the Good Samaritan is one of the most familiar and beloved stories in the Bible. We sometimes forget how radical this teaching of Jesus would have been to his first listeners. They would not have used the words "good" and "Samaritan" in the same sentence. Jews and Samaritans were historically very close to one another, but sometimes those closest to us can be the ones who cause us the most hurt.

In Jesus' story, a man was beaten and stripped of his clothes—his identity. When he was lying there beside the road, those passing could not tell who he was or to which social or cultural group he belonged. Anyone who stopped to help him would have to be someone who was willing to stop and help anybody, without concern for who he was. The Samaritan was the one who chose to show mercy, even to a complete stranger. Jesus made the one who was the hated outsider to be the example of true faithfulness.

The challenge is not in remembering this very familiar story, but in having the courage to follow Jesus' teaching here and to live it. Who are the neighbors that are difficult for you to love? As a Christian, what do you do to try to love them? Have you seen God's grace working in someone that others look down on? 🌱

19. "Who Is My Neighbor?"

"Who is my neighbor?" a lawyer asked Jesus, to test him.
So Jesus told him a story to answer his question:
Lonely the way . . .
Lonely the traveler one day . . .
Robbers attacked him and left him.

First down the road came a priest who just chose to ignore him.
Next came a Levite who wouldn't do anything for him.
Then one despised,
Hated in everyone's eyes,
Knelt down to heal and restore him.

Tending the wounds of the man, the Samaritan labored.
He was the one with compassion, the one in God's favor.
Not by a creed
But by responding to need,
He proved to be the good neighbor.

Tune: LOBE DEN HERREN 14 14.478 ("Praise Ye the Lord, the Almighty"), *Stralsund Erneuerten Gesangbuch*, 1665.

Christ Taught Us of a Farmer

When St. Paul's Lutheran Church in Warren, Illinois, was preparing to celebrate its 100th anniversary, the congregation wanted a hymn for the occasion. I wrote this hymn for that special time in the church's life and ministry. Since Warren is a farming community, Jesus' parable of the sower going out to sow seemed to be a most appropriate theme. See Mark 4:1-20, Matthew 13:1-13, and Luke 8:4-15.

All churches—in rural areas, in the suburbs, or in the city—can relate to Jesus' story of the sower. We all like to see the fruits of our labors.

Someone once commented that pastors do a lot of work for which they may never see visible results. We preach on Sunday mornings—and wonder how our words make a difference in people's Monday-through-Saturday lives. We baptize, we teach confirmation classes, we listen to people who are experiencing difficult times, we visit people in the hospital (including strangers we are asked to see). In all these things, we wonder, "What happens to the seeds we plant? Will something I've said or done make a difference? How?"

As congregations, we celebrate the sacraments. We welcome new members. We invite people to join us for worship and Church school. We reach out into the community in the summer with vacation Bible school. We try new programs and ministries. Will something we have said or done make a difference? How?

We all plant seeds in our everyday living. We all have opportunities to join in caring conversations, to pray for others, to help lonely neighbors, to reach out to people who are hurting. The question is: do the things we do really make a difference?

Sometimes the things we try may fail; sometimes the good news lands on rocky soil. But we all know the joy when the seeds of faith take root and grow. How have you witnessed seeds of faith growing recently? In the end, we remember it's not our crop that we're bringing in. And so we pray, "Your harvest is for sharing; sent out, we work for you."

20. Christ Taught Us of a Farmer

Christ taught us of a farmer who went out sowing seeds.
A few had trouble growing among the rocks and weeds.
But others grew till harvest in soil that was so good.
O God, you sow the gospel: The seed is your own word.

You sowed your word of love here so many years ago.*
Your message found a welcome; your word began to grow.
By grace, this church was built here by saints who followed you.
The seed took root and flourished: we hear and follow, too.

We thank you for each member who lives in loving ways,
For those who seek to serve you without expecting praise.
For hearts and songs uplifted, for work and sacrifice.
The seed you planted grows here: we grow in Jesus Christ.

In times of joy we praise you, in struggling times we search,
And always we are learning to be your faithful church.
Your Spirit gives us vision, and hearts and lives made new.
Your harvest is for sharing: sent out, we work for you.

*Original wording was "You sowed your word of love here one hundred years ago."

Tune: AURELIA 76.76 D ("The Church's One Foundation"), Samuel Sebastian Wesley, 1864.
Text: Copyright © 2000 by Carolyn Winfrey Gillette. All rights reserved.

Christ, You Walked Among the Grain Fields

This hymn was commissioned by Susan Ryan, Executive Director of Presbyterian Disaster Assistance. She served on the Board for the Food Resource Bank, and asked that a hymn be written for that organization and in gratitude for Norm Braksick's faithful service with the Food Resource Bank. The hymn is based on several biblical texts: Matthew 13:1-23; Mark 4:1-9, 26-29; and Luke 8:4-15.

As Jesus traveled the land, teaching people about God's kingdom, he used stories of farming, stories of "the land." We are called to see the connections between land and faith, both in Jesus' parables and in the places we live. As we look around our land of plenty, we see the disparity between those who have more than enough and those who can barely survive. I remember sitting in an open-air restaurant in a city in Honduras, at the end of a long, hot mission trip. We were looking forward to a good dinner after a particularly challenging week.

As we began to eat, little children reached their thin arms through the bars of the gates of that open-air restaurant, saying in Spanish, "I am hungry." We shared our food that day, but we sadly realized that what we gave would only help those children for a day. The next day, they would be hungry again. Their words, and the words of millions of children like them, need to inspire us as Christians to reach out to our neighbors near and far. Jesus cared—and he cares today—about people's stomachs being full as well as about their faith being rich and wonderful. The church is called to work for a world where everyone can experience God's feast, in mind, body and spirit.

Are you a "city friend" or a "country neighbor"? How can you work with others of different backgrounds to make the world a more just and caring place? Can you lend expertise or land, or can you give money? Our local church food closet invites people with gardens to donate fresh produce to be distributed along with canned and boxed foods. Are there ways you can learn more about the needs of hungry neighbors in the world? What can you do to "even things out" between your own lifestyle and that of people in great need?

21. Christ, You Walked Among the Grain Fields

Christ, you walked among the grain fields, Finding lessons all around:
"Like the harvest that the earth yields, So God's kingdom will abound."
"See! A sower goes out planting; Some seed grows a hundredfold."
Here on earth you gave us heaven In the stories that you told.

Lord, you shared God's kingdom-bounty, Yet you know our pain and need.
Some are poor in lands of plenty, Often hurt by others' greed.
Some, possessed by their possessions, Look for more to buy and keep;
Others long for simpler blessings: "Let my hungry children eat."

Lord, you send us out to labor, To pass on the love you give;
City friend and country neighbor Work as one so all may live.
Lending land and tools and vision, Sharing costs and planting seed—
Work we love becomes our mission As we serve your world in need.

May our harvest celebration Build new food security;
As we care for your creation, May we find community.
By your Holy Spirit bless us And may what we grow increase
Till the whole world sees new glimpses Of your joyful banquet feast.

Tune: BEACH SPRING 87.87 D ("God, Whose Giving Knows No Ending"), *The Sacred Harp*, 1844
Text: Copyright © 2005 by Carolyn Winfrey Gillette. All rights reserved.

Where Is Bread?

"Where Is Bread?" was written on the train from Philadelphia to Boston when I was traveling to a hymn conference. This hymn celebrates the only miracle that is found in all four gospels (the feeding of the five thousand: see Matthew 14:13-21, Mark 6:32-44, Luke 9:10-17 and John 6:1-15). Jesus meets our physical as well as spiritual needs in his holistic ministry; the church is called to do the same. The hymn text, formatted together with the music, can be found in *Christian Reflection,* the journal of the Center for Christian Ethics at Baylor University: <http://www3.baylor.edu/christianethics/FoodandHunger hymnGillette.pdf>.

When Jesus was faced with a crowd of hungry people, he had compassion on them and gave them food to take care of their physical hunger. Jesus, the Bread of Life, cared for the needs of hungry people.

We hunger, too, though many of us don't hunger for food. We are over-stuffed with possessions and hunger for Life. I remember working as a summer intern in one community with absolutely beautiful homes; some of the residents hated to go out at night because they didn't want to leave their very expensive houses behind. There had been a rash of robberies in their neighborhood that year. They were afraid someone might break in while they were away at a church meeting or a social gathering, so they stayed home. They gave up a sense of community to hold onto the things they owned.

I met another person, a member of a different church, who had been fighting with her family over an inheritance and had not spoken to them for years because of how possessions had been divided. It is easy to become possessed by possessions. Yet the things we own won't satisfy us in the end. We need the Bread of Life.

In the world around us, we hear cries of hunger from the millions of people in our world who don't have enough to eat. When the disciples came to Jesus and said, "The people are hungry," Jesus told them, "You give them something to eat." As Christians obeying the call of Jesus to help our hungry neighbors, we find our richest blessings in reaching out and serving others. "Give us bread and help us share it" is a prayer for others and for us, too.

22. Where Is Bread?

"Where is bread?" the great crowd murmured—
Thousands strong, yet all in need.
"Where is bread?" your people wondered,
Faced with such a crowd to feed.
Who, Lord Jesus, could have guessed it?
One small boy brought food to share.
Taking what he gave, you blessed it;
All were fed, with much to spare.

Where is bread? We know their yearning;
Every day, we wish for more.
God, in time, we're slowly learning:
All we own can make us poor.
Our possessions can possess us,
Leaving hunger deep inside.
Christ our Bread, come now and bless us;
At your feast, we're satisfied.

"Where is bread?" the call is rising;
Millions cry who must be fed.
God, your answer seems surprising:
"You, my Church, you give them bread."
Bread to fill each hungry spirit,
Bread for hungry stomachs, too!
Give us bread and help us share it.
Richly blest, may we serve you.

Tune: ABBOT'S LEIGH 87.87 D *("God Is Here!")*, Cyril Vincent Taylor, 1941.
Alternate tune: IN BABILONE
Text: Copyright © 2000 by Carolyn Winfrey Gillette. All rights reserved.

Do Not Turn Away the Children

Biblical texts for this hymn include: Matthew 19:13-15; Mark 9:33-37; Mark 10:13-16; and Luke 18:15-17. The hymn in its original version includes the line: "Do not turn your back on children hungry, hunted in Darfur." My prayer is that by the time this book is published, the crisis in that part of the world will have ended. An alternate line is "Do not turn your back on children who know violence, pain and war."

One of the pictures that I remember seeing on the wall of just about every church I attended as a child was a picture of Jesus blessing the children. While this scene makes a beautiful framed print, we forget how surprising Jesus' words and actions must have seemed to his disciples. Children in that day were among the groups of people who had low social standing. They were supposed to stay out of the way, at the very least. Yet Jesus welcomed the children, as he did others who were on the fringes of society.

Our society says it honors children, but in many ways children are still on the outside looking in. Countless children and teenagers remain in foster care with no one to say, "You are my child!" When they become eighteen years old, some of them are sent out to fend for themselves with little or no community support. Incredible numbers of children and youth around the world suffer and die from AIDS, without medicine. Many communities regularly vote down school referendums, and children miss out on quality education. Still other children want to have their faith questions taken seriously, yet they may find their joys and wonders are overlooked by busy adults.

We know what Jesus taught and how he lived. How does he call us, in love, to welcome children in our world today? Who are the children near by and far away who need to hear his welcome? How does your church reach out to welcome them in Jesus' name?

23. Do Not Turn Away the Children

"Do not turn away the children.
Let them come to me instead,
For to them belongs the kingdom.
Make them welcome!" Christ, you said.
As we hear your words of blessing
That you spoke when they drew near,
Can we hear your love addressing
Needs of children we see here?

Do not turn your back on children
Hungry, hunted in Darfur;*
Give them justice, food and welcome,
Make their homes and lives secure.
Don't neglect the world of children
Who have AIDS and HIV,
For to them belongs the kingdom.
Give them health care that they need.

Do not tell the nation's children,
"Schools are what we can't afford!"
Give them all good education;
Teach them well, both rich and poor.
Do not hurry past the children
Longing for your love this day;
For to them belongs the kingdom;
Give them time, don't turn away.

Do not miss the faith of children
Who have questions deep inside,
For to them belongs the kingdom;
Wonder with them, be their guide.
Jesus, as we hear your blessing
For those ones you welcomed in,
May our deeds reflect your caring
As we welcome them again!

*Alternative wording, "Who know violence, pain and war."

Tune: BEACH SPRING 87.87 D ("God, Whose Giving Knows No Ending"), *The Sacred Harp*, 1844
Text: Copyright © 2007 by Carolyn Winfrey Gillette. All rights reserved.

O Lord, As You Were On Your Way

This hymn was requested by friends in Australia, John and Val Fizzell. Biblical references for this transfiguration hymn include Matthew 17:1-13, Mark 9:2-13, Luke 9:28-36, and 2 Peter 1:16-18.

Jesus' transfiguration is a mystery. Sometimes all we can do is tell the story again and again in amazement. What we may understand best in the story is the disciples' longing to make that moment last. They wanted to hang onto the glory, preserve the excitement, and stay on the mountaintop.

Summer church camp was always a mountaintop experience for me when I was growing up. Mission trips and church retreats have been wonderful times of getting away over the years. Christmas candlelight services and Easter morning worship celebrations bring me great joy. All of us are moved by those "thin places" that are referred to in Celtic spirituality—the places where earth and heaven come so close together.

Yet, Jesus teaches us again and again that if we want to follow him, we need to get back to the valleys of service. We need to go back to the committee meetings, the soup kitchens, the children who need tutoring, the crying babies, the letters that need to be written to leaders in Congress, the neighbors' homes that need to be repaired, the sick relatives who need to be cared for, and the sacrifices that need to be made in serving others.

What can we learn from Jesus, about what it means to "choose the harder way"?

24. O Lord, As You Were On Your Way

O Lord, as you were on your way to where you'd one day die,
You wanted time to rest and pray, to hear God's word to you that day.
You climbed a mountain high with three good friends close by.

So soon, the three became aware of such a wondrous sight.
Your face shone bright beyond compare, just like a glimpse of heaven there!
Your clothes were dazzling white; your glory came to light.

The Law, the Prophets guided you as you discerned God's will.
With Moses and Elijah, too, you spoke of God's great plan for you,
God's promise to fulfill, one Friday on a hill.

Why could you not remain with them and there in glory stay?
God said, "This is my own dear Son! Now listen to him, everyone!"
And so you turned to say you'd go the harder way.

O Lord, how often we pursue success at any cost,
And yet we hear God's word anew, that we are called to follow you,
Who served the poor and lost and journeyed to the cross.

Tune: REPTON 86.886 ("How Clear Is Our Vocation, Lord"), C. Hubert H. Parry, 1888

When Mary Poured a Rich Perfume

The biblical story for this hymn is found in John 12:1-8, and Jesus makes reference to Deuteronomy 15:11. See also Matthew 26:6-13 and Mark 14:3-9.

Faithful people in Jesus' day memorized many passages of scripture. Jesus, and the gospel writers, would often quote part of a verse with the expectation that people would know what followed. The same thing happens today when Christians hear the phrase, "Our Father, who art in heaven. . . ." Most of us naturally think of what follows— "Hallowed be thy name." When people hear the beginning of some well-known saying, they can fill in the rest of the words.

Sometimes people misuse the verse from the Bible that says, "The poor you will always have with you." Since the Bible says this, they argue, they do not need to help those who are living in poverty. The words of scripture become an excuse for doing nothing.

Yet what Jesus was quoting to Judas was Deuteronomy 15:11: "Since there will never cease to be some in need on the earth, *I therefore command you, 'Open your hand to the poor and needy neighbor in your land'*" (emphasis added). Rather than saying there is nothing we should do about the poor, the Bible makes clear in the second half of this verse that we are called to help those in need. When Jesus quoted "The poor you will always have with you," his followers would have known immediately the command that followed to "open your hand."

The hymn asks, "O Christ, what can your people bring to show you thanks and love?" When we celebrate Jesus' birth, can we do it by giving gifts to the poor in honor of loved ones who already have enough? Many Christians are finding new ways to do this at Christmas and other times by giving alternative gifts that help people who are in need.

We live surrounded by the poor and needy of the land; do we live with clenched fists or open hands?

25. When Mary Poured a Rich Perfume

When Mary poured a rich perfume on Jesus' weary feet,
Her caring filled that humble room; the fragrance there was sweet.
But full of anger, Judas said, "We could have used this more!
Why was her gift not sold instead, and given to the poor?"

The Lord replied, "Leave her alone! She bought it for this day.
This caring love that she has shown is faithful to God's way.
The poor will always be with you, but you will not have me."
He blessed her and he thanked her, too, for giving lavishly.

O Christ, what can your people bring to show you thanks and love?
You need no fragrant offering; for now you reign above.
Since there will never cease to be the poor throughout the land,
May we, your church, serve faithfully by offering them our hand.

Tune: ELLACOMBE 76.76 D ("Hail to the Lord's Anointed"), *Gesangbuch der Herzogl, Wirtembergischen Katholischen Hofkapelle*, 1784; alt. 1868
Alternate Tune: FOREST GREEN ("All Beautiful the March of Days")
Text: Copyright © 2001 by Carolyn Winfrey Gillette. All rights reserved.

Jesus Sat and Watched the Crowd

This hymn text and tune formatted together are available at the United Methodist Church's Center for Worship Resourcing web site (<www.gbod.org/worship>). It is based on the story of the widow's offering. See Mark 12:41-44 and Luke 21:1-4.

One of the wonderful Bible stories that many children learn in church school is "the widow's mite." It is one of the first stories we learn and perhaps one of the hardest to accept. As adults, we argue with the text: "Who would take care of her, if she gave everything away? Is it practical to give away everything? Isn't careful planning and saving a better approach?"

We know there were other times that Jesus praised people for extravagant generosity. For example, Jesus commended Zacchaeus after he told Jesus, "Look, half of my possessions, Lord, I will give to the poor; and if I have defrauded anyone of anything, I will pay back four times as much" (Luke 19:8). Jesus knew that a willingness to give generously to God and to others witnessed to a person's trust in God.

Sometimes people are reluctant to give to the church because they are not happy with how every penny is being spent by the institution. It is interesting that Jesus had problems with the Temple and yet he did not allow that to become an excuse for not giving to God. Jesus still commended the woman for her faithful and sacrificial gift.

God knows what is in our hearts and our wallets. And we probably know, deep inside, that giving generously and trusting God completely will lead to the richness that the widow knew when she gave everything she had:

"Trusting you, our gifts will grow
And our joy will overflow."

26. Jesus Sat and Watched the Crowd

Jesus sat and watched the crowd
At the temple treasury.
Some that day were rich and proud,
Making sure that all could see
Their great generosity.

Then a widow came along
Who had nothing she could spare.
Yet her faith in God was strong
And she gave as few would dare:
All she had, she chose to share.

Just a penny, nothing more,
Yet Christ said her gift was best.
What a risk, for one so poor!
What rich faith her gift expressed!
Trusting, giving, she was blest.

Lord, you see the way we live;
All within our hearts, you know.
Like that widow, may we give.
Trusting you, our gifts will grow
And our joy will overflow.

Tune: HENDON 77.77.7 ("Take My Life" and "Ask Ye What Great Thing I Know"), H.A. Cesar Malan, 1827

Our Lord, You Stood in Pilate's Hall

This hymn is appropriate for Christ the King Sunday and for days in the church year when we especially contemplate Jesus' suffering and death leading to his resurrection and reign in glory. See Matthew 27:1-2,11-26; Mark 15:1-15; Luke 23:1-25; John 18:28-19:6 and Matthew 26:52-56.

To ordinary people looking on, Jesus must have seemed insignificant as he stood before mighty Pilate; through the eyes of faith we see Christ "at the right hand of God" ruling over all creation. Though we know Christ as ruler of all, there are plenty of times when we ask, "When will your reign be known?" Another way of asking this might be, "Why are we still suffering if you have already won, Lord?" A woman struggles to care for an elderly relative; a father waits at the hospital for news of his son who has been shot; a child waits in a long line for one bowl of food to fend off her hunger for a while; children and their families hide in shelters from the violence outside. "When will your reign be known?"

At the same time, Christians in comfortable churches, with comfortable lives, pray, "Thy kingdom come, thy will be done. . . ." We pray not to get so caught up in the comfortable ways of our culture that we lose sight of something more precious. "Lord, may we not forget your Way, nor lose your kingdom's song." We pray that we may seek God's kingdom first, and most of all.

27. Our Lord, You Stood in Pilate's Hall

Our Lord, you stood in Pilate's hall,
His judgment to endure.
Yet all he ruled would one day fall;
You reign forevermore!

You are our King and yet you said
It's not by sword or might;
Where truth is lived and love is spread,
Your reign comes into sight.

Where people live in deep despair,
Forgotten, hurt, alone,
We hear their urgent, whispered prayer:
"When will your reign be known?"

And where your church on earth today
Is mighty, rich and strong,
Lord, may we not forget your Way,
Nor lose your kingdom's song.

"Thy kingdom come, thy will be done"
Not just in heaven above;
O God, may we obey your Son,
Who reigns o'er all in love.

Tune: AZMON CM ("O For a Thousand Tongues to Sing"), Carl Gotthelf Gläser, 1828, arr. Lowell Mason, 1839

Peter Said, "I'm Going Fishing"

This hymn was commissioned for a celebration of the fiftieth anniversary of the Little Chapel on the Boardwalk, in Wrightsville Beach, North Carolina. It is based on John 21:1-14. The third line of the last verse of the hymn, written for that church by the ocean, was "In our worship, in our giving, In our serving by the sea." "In our worship, in our giving, in our serving those in need" is the revised version of that line for inland congregations.

There are times when we step out in faith and things don't go at all the way we had planned. There are times when we find ourselves in such unfamiliar territory that we just need to go back to something we know. Peter and the other disciples knew what it meant to have experiences like these. After Jesus' death, they were surely heartbroken and confused. After Jesus' resurrection, they were in completely new territory and were not sure what to do. So, Peter did what was most familiar to him; he went back to fishing. It was there in the fishing boat that Jesus appeared to Peter and the others and called them to continue his ministry. "Feed my sheep," Jesus told Peter.

In the church, we often fall into familiar patterns of doing ministry—sometimes because we are afraid, but often because it is simply the easiest thing to do. We like the familiar. Then the risen Christ sends us fishing again. Then he shows us something new that we could be doing.

When we arrived at the church we are currently serving, there were a lot of heavy metal and rock concerts being held at the Grange Hall next door to the church. On warm spring and summer evenings, teenagers would park in the church parking lot and hang out there during the concerts, and church members were concerned about some of the activities that seemed to be happening there. Instead of running the youth off church property, several church members began going to the church on concert nights; they opened up the church gym, served some refreshments, and brought a couple of guitars. They invited the youth who were hanging out in the parking lot to come into the church, for a break from the hectic pace of the concert next door. A ministry of hospitality began. "Cast your nets where I have told you," Jesus says. Where is God guiding your church into new areas of ministry?

28. Peter Said, "I'm Going Fishing"

Peter said, "I'm going fishing," so his friends went out with him.
Through the night, they labored, watching, Hauling empty nets back in.
In the grey of early morning, Jesus, you came walking by.
From the beach you called a greeting, "Cast out on the other side!"

Soon their nets were filled to brimming; Someone cried, "It is the Lord!"
Jumping in, he started swimming; Christ, you met him on the shore.
Guiding them to better waters, Eating fish and sharing bread,
You showed Peter and the others: You were risen from the dead!

Risen Christ, you send us fishing! God's great sea is everywhere.
You have guided us in mission, You have given love to share.
Through the years, our church has heard you, We have answered your great call:
"Cast your nets where I have told you. Bring my word of love to all!"

Lord, be with our congregation; By your Spirit, send us forth!
May we care for your creation, May we work for peace on earth.
In our worship, in our giving, In our serving those in need,
May we know, Lord; you are living, Guiding us in ministry.

Tune: BEECHER 87.87 D ("Love Divine, All Loves Excelling"), John Zundel, 1870
Alternate Tunes: HYMN TO JOY, ABBOT'S LEIGH

O Christ, When You Ascended

The ascension of Jesus is a topic that we don't talk about very much in church, even though we affirm it every time we say the words of the Apostles' Creed: "He ascended into heaven." In writing this hymn, I found some helpful ideas in the writings of John Calvin, John McClure, and N.T. Wright. See Acts 1:1-11 and Luke 24:44-53.

The ascension of Jesus doesn't mean that Jesus leaves us; it means he is present to us in a new way, through God's Spirit, and through his prayers for us. Christ is no longer limited by the things that limit the rest of us; he reigns over everything. He is no longer simply Jesus of the past; he is with us today.

Philippians 2:10-11 proclaims that one day "at the name of Jesus every knee should bend, in heaven and on earth and under the earth, and every tongue should confess that Jesus Christ is Lord, to the glory of God the Father." One day . . . one day . . . one day . . . Christ's reign will be fully known. Until then, we wait and hope, and look forward to the day when all heaven and earth will celebrate together.

Read Acts 1:1-11. What does Jesus' ascension mean to you? How are we tempted to leave Jesus "in stories nicely told"? How have you experienced the presence of Jesus in your life and in the church? 🌱

29. O Christ, When You Ascended

O Christ, when you ascended, you took your rightful throne.
Your time on earth had ended—yet we weren't left alone.
You reign o'er earth and heaven; your Spirit guides our way.
Your prayers uphold your people; you lead your church each day.

We look at earthly rulers and see what they command.
We note their years of power, the borders of their land.
Yet, Lord, you are not bounded by things like time and space;
Your reign is never-ending, you rule in every place.

We're tempted. Lord, to leave you in stories nicely told.
Sometimes we don't believe you and say your ways are old.
Sometimes we feel so lonely and live in doubt and fear—
But your ascension means, Lord, you're present with us here.

It's often quite a challenge to follow in your Way.
We're easily distracted! It's hard, Lord, to obey.
Sometimes we give you Sundays—an hour, maybe two—
But your ascension means, Lord, all life belongs to you.

One day, O Lord, we'll know you, as we are fully known.
One day this world of sinners will bow before your throne.
One day, God's whole creation will sing and praise your name.
On earth as now in heaven, we'll celebrate your reign.

Tune: LANCASHIRE 76.76 D ("The Day of Resurrection!"), Henry Thomas Smart, 1835.
Text: Copyright © 2007 by Carolyn Winfrey Gillette. All rights reserved.

Listen, Sisters! Listen, Brothers!

The Rev. Dr. Charles (Buz) Myers gave a Bible study series on 1 Corinthians at Massanetta Springs Conference Center. This hymn is based on what Myers shared in that class, especially about 1 Corinthians 15. The central theme of this hymn can be found in the third line: "We have life in Jesus' name." See also Romans 5:12-21.

As I was working on this particular text, our fourteen-year-old daughter, Sarah, came by and looked over my shoulder to see what I was doing. She joyfully said to me, "Mom, that's the theme of Harry Potter!" I asked her what she was talking about, and she said, "That one line of your hymn summarizes all the Harry Potter books: 'Love has conquered, death can't win.'" That's a pretty good lesson for a fictional story to be teaching our children. It is all the better when our Christian faith teaches children (and all of us) this same lesson in real life. God loves us so much in Jesus Christ that God's love triumphs over everything, even death itself.

In addition to serving as a pastor, I have worked in three different communities as a hospice chaplain. It has been a privilege to work with hospice nurses and other staff members; they are among the most caring people I know.

Working with hospice patients has helped me to treasure the Christian faith that is so much a part of my life. Everything else about faith hinges on what is found in 1 Corinthians 15—a belief in resurrection through our Lord Jesus Christ.

> "What could be our proclamation
> If our Lord had not been raised,
> For without his resurrection,
> What could give hope to our days?
> But in fact, our Christ is living . . ."

Jesus' resurrection means there is hope for you and me.

Jesus' resurrection means that God's kingdom is coming, and we're called to hope for it and work for it now.

Jesus' resurrection means that life is not futile; there is long-term meaning in our struggle for peace and justice, even if we don't see all the results right now.

Jesus' resurrection means that we are free to take risks for our faith here and now.

Jesus' resurrection means that a family can say good-bye to a loved one who has been suffering for so long, knowing that good-bye means just for a while.

Jesus' resurrection means that a hospice patient can yell and holler at God but know that, in the end, she is safe in God's arms forever.

30. Listen, Sisters! Listen, Brothers!

Listen, sisters! Listen, brothers!
To the news that we proclaim;
Spread the word and tell your neighbors:
We have life in Jesus' name.
All because God loves us dearly,
Jesus died for all our sin.
On the third day, God showed clearly:
Love has conquered, death can't win.

What could be our proclamation
If our Lord had not been raised,
For without his resurrection,
What could give hope to our days?
But in fact, our Christ is living—
First to live, of those who've died;
For as all are lost through Adam,
So in Christ, we're made alive.

What is sown will surely perish;
What is raised will still endure.
What is sown is sown in weakness;
What is raised will die no more.
Flesh and blood cannot inherit
That great kingdom God will bring.
God will change us—never fear it!
Death, defeated, has no sting.

Tune: BEACH SPRING 87.87 D ("God Whose Giving Knows No Ending"), *The Sacred Harp.* 1844.
Text: Copyright © 2006 by Carolyn Winfrey Gillette. All rights reserved.

For Freedom, Christ Has Set Us Free

This hymn was written at the Synod School of the PC(USA) Synod of the Trinity (Pennsylvania, and portions of Ohio and West Virginia), after a class that was taught by Dr. Charles Myers on Galatians. It lifts up some of the wonderful themes of that New Testament letter.

Galatians reminds us that all the work we do to justify ourselves in the sight of God comes to nothing, and then God reaches out and says, "My child! You belong to me!" Specifically, Galatians 4:4-7 puts it this way: "But when the fullness of time had come, God sent his Son, born of a woman, born under the law, in order to redeem those who were under the law, so that we might receive adoption as children."

What a wonderful gift it is for any child without a home to be adopted by a loving parent or parents. Adoption websites often highlight children in need of homes by saying, "This child is looking forward to having a 'forever home' and a 'forever family.'" We have a forever home and a forever family because of God's love for us in Jesus Christ.

The last verse of this hymn points to the "fruit of the Spirit" found in Galatians 5:22-23: "The fruit of the Spirit is love, joy, peace, patience, kindness, generosity, faithfulness, gentleness, and self-control." What is it like, for you, to have a new identity in Jesus Christ? What fruit are you bearing because of God's love today?

31. For Freedom, Christ Has Set Us Free!

"For freedom, Christ has set us free!"
What joy is ours to claim!
No more enslaved, humanity
Finds life in Jesus' name.
We try, Lord, to be justified
Through all the works we do.
Yet you adopt us, saying, "Child,
It's Christ who makes you new."

We're clothed in Christ and we belong;
Now no one waits outside.
In him we find our common song;
Old ways no more divide.
"It is no longer I who live,
But Christ who lives in me."
He died for us, new life to give—
And new identity.

Now, Spirit-filled, may we be led
From ways that would destroy.
May we your people turn instead
To lives of love and joy.
May we find peace that makes us whole
And patience everywhere.
God, give us kindness, self-control,
And hearts and hands that share.

Tune: ELLACOMBE 76.76 D ("I Sing the Mighty Power of God"), *Gesangbuch der Herzogl. Wirtembergisch, Katholischen Hofkapelle*, 1784; alt. 1868

Text: Copyright © 2000 by Carolyn Winfrey Gillette. All rights reserved.

We Hear, Lord, Your Promise

Kit Schooley asked if I had written a hymn on 2 Corinthians 12:5-10, a passage he planned to preach on at the Bryn Mawr Presbyterian Church. It is that beautiful passage that inspired this song.

As a hospice chaplain and as a pastor, I have been with many people who have dealt with incredible suffering. While we cannot answer the question, "Why?" we can find great comfort that God is with us in times of pain and hurt.

Biblical scholars have speculated for generations about what Paul's thorn in the flesh was—whether it was physical, psychological or spiritual. We simply don't know, other than to say that it was a source of pain for him, and that he asked God many times to relieve his suffering.

A few weeks ago, my husband and co-pastor Bruce and I were serving the Lord's Supper to the congregation with people coming forward to receive the sacrament. One by one they came down the center aisle, and as we watched them come forward, we were reminded of some of the things they had been going through—a painful illness, heart surgery, a death in the family, a miscarriage, a troubled relationship, or a work-related concern. As I said to each person, "The body of Christ, broken for you . . ." I also remembered Jesus' promises: "I am with you always" and "My grace is sufficient."

32. We Hear, Lord, Your Promise

We hear, Lord, your promise: "My grace is sufficient!"
Those few simple words brought such comfort to Paul;
And though every thorn in the flesh may be different
We find in your message good news for us all.
Your strength is made perfect in times of our weakness,
When hardships assail us and pain comes along.
For you dwell within us and we learn your goodness—
And when we are weakest, in you we are strong.

Through all that we suffer, your grace is a blessing;
O Christ, you are with us to carry us through.
What hope you still offer when life is distressing!
You heal and forgive us, so we turn to you.
When pain is so great that we hardly can bear it,
We call on your name and we hear your love's song;
You send us the comfort and peace of your Spirit,
And when we are weakest, in you we are strong.

Tune: ASH GROVE 12.11.12.11 D ("Let All Things Now Living"), Welsh folk melody
Text: Copyright © 2007 by Carolyn Winfrey Gillette. All rights reserved.

No Longer

This hymn is based on Galatians 3:23-29. It was written at the request of the Rev. Dr. Jacqueline E. Taylor, then Moderator of the Synod of the Mid-Atlantic of the Presbyterian Church (USA). The hymn was sung for the first time at the Synod's annual meeting at Westminster Presbyterian Church in Wilmington, Delaware.

The early church struggled with divisiveness, even as the church does today. The radical nature of God's grace that Paul talks about in Galatians 3:28 is a message for today as much as it was for the first readers of his letter. God's love in Jesus Christ not only overcomes the barriers between humanity and God, but also calls for an end to the barriers between people, especially in the Christian church.

Once when I was in Honduras after Hurricane Mitch—a storm that killed thousands of people there—a church worker in a rural community said to me, "Some North American churches seem to worry and fight about the most unusual things. I think it is better to spend our time and energy feeding the children who are hungry. I think that is what God would want us to do."

One of the problems with divisiveness and conflict in the church is that while we are trying to solve it, the world goes right on by. We lose opportunities for reaching out to children, youth and young adults. We overlook evangelism needs. We make mission a lower priority than it should be. On the other hand, when we work as one body of Christ, "the life we live together is an answered prayer."

33. No Longer

No longer Jew or Greek, no longer slave or free—
In you, O Christ, we're given wondrous unity.
Here in your church we learn that nothing can divide;
Here men and women, called by God, serve side by side.

No longer in your church should there be rich or poor—
You taught us kingdom values worth our struggling for.
Here some have wealth to give, and some, great faith to share.
The life we live together is an answered prayer.

No longer left or right, defending our own case—
O God, we're sinners in your sight, in need of grace.
The common bond we know is Christ who sets us free;
In Christ we live and love and grow in unity.

O God, we look around and know (each one) our guilt;
By your own Spirit, now break down the walls we've built.
When we were all baptized, we died to our old ways;
A church diverse, yet one in Christ, we give you praise.

Tune: LEONI 66.84 D ("The God of Abraham Praise"), Hebrew melody, adapt. Thomas Olivers and Meyer Lyon, 1770.

The Fruit of the Spirit

This hymn was inspired by Paul's beautiful image of how the Holy Spirit bears fruit in Christian lives. It was written to help Christians of all ages learn and celebrate the fruit of the Spirit found in Galatians 5:22-23.

"The fruit of the Spirit is love, joy, peace, patience, kindness, generosity, faithfulness, gentleness, and self-control" (Galatians 5:22-23). What do our lives look like when we are filled with the fruit of the Spirit? Which of these things is the hardest for you to have in your life? 🌱

34. The Fruit of the Spirit

The fruit of the Spirit is love for our sharing,
It's joy in the gospel that we have from you.
It's peace that we live out with courage and daring;
It's patience, for we know that we have sinned, too.
It's kindness in all things and generous giving;
Its faithfulness seeking to follow your way.
It's gentleness, Lord, and it's self-controlled living;
Now make us more fruitful in these things, we pray.

Tune: ASH GROVE 6 6.11.6 6.11 D ("Let All Things Now Living"), Welsh folk melody.
Text: Copyright © 2006 by Carolyn Winfrey Gillette. All rights reserved.

Be Doers of the Word of God

This hymn was written at the Synod of the Trinity's Synod School, after a class by the Rev. Dr. Charles Myers. "Be Doers of the Word of God" is primarily based on a wonderful passage from James 1-2 that talks about "true religion." See also Ephesians 2:7-8, Ephesians 5:1-2 and 1 John 3:18, 23.

Once a woman stopped by our church and asked, "Would I be allowed to come to worship in sweatpants and a t-shirt?" We assured her that she would be welcome. She explained her reason for asking: she had been discouraged from attending another church when she had showed up in those clothes. She said she wasn't trying to be disrespectful, but that was all she had. "Religion that is pure and undefiled before God, the Father, is this: to care for orphans and widows in their distress, and to keep oneself unstained by the world" (James 1:27). James 2:1-7 goes on to talk about not showing favoritism to the people who come into church. We don't honor finely-dressed Christians and send away those who are poor.

Many times when we talk about faith, we emphasize the importance of God's grace (found, for example, in Ephesians 2:8 and 5:1-2, which are the basis of the third verse of the hymn), or we talk about the importance of what we believe. These are important things! Yet James nudges us all to put our faith into action and to care for the outcasts, the poor, and those in need.

35. Be Doers of the Word of God

Be doers of the word of God,
Not simply those who hear.
Be ones who look into God's word,
Obey, and persevere.
Be quick to listen, slow to speak,
And slow to anger, too.
Put wrath aside; instead, be meek
And let God work in you.

Religion that is undefiled,
Religion that is pure
Will reach to help the orphaned child
And welcome all the poor.
If people come here poorly dressed,
To judge them is a sin.
The rich aren't better than the rest;
God welcomes poor ones in.

O Christ, you save us by God's grace
From having to obey.
Then freed to love, we can embrace
A life that seeks your way.
May we be doers of the word,
May faith shine through our deeds;
And as we seek to trust in God,
May ethics follow creeds.

Tune: ELLACOMBE 76.76 D ("I Sing the Mighty Power of God"), *Gesangbuch der Herzogl, Wirtembergischen, Katholischen Hofkapelle,* 1784; alt. 1868

Worship

O God, You Made the Sabbath Day

This hymn was inspired by a Presbyterian General Assembly study on the Sabbath. Several books have recently been written by Dorothy Bass, Walter Muller, Don Postema and others on the importance of Sabbath. The renewed interest in spiritual practice and disciplines may also renew our interest in the ancient practice of Sabbath for rest and worship. Biblical references for this hymn include Exodus 20:11, Deuteronomy 5:15; Acts 20:7; and 2 Corinthians 5:17.

Many older people in the churches I have served have expressed concern that Sabbath days today are not what they used to be. They remember the Blue laws that used to prohibit many kinds of shopping and recreation on Sundays. Some people, on the other hand, remember Sundays as oppressive times, when children couldn't go outside to play and have fun. As Christians from different backgrounds and generations, we have different experiences with Sabbath.

Sabbath time is meant to be a "freeing gift." It is part of the pattern of our lives, where rest follows work. Sabbath is a gracious gift from a loving God; if we accept this gift, our lives are changed and renewed.

As Christians, we worship on Sundays because every Sunday is a little Easter celebration, remembering that Christ is risen. Every Sunday is a time to praise God for his wonderful gift to us in Jesus Christ, to worship, to rest, to be reminded that we are human and can't do it all, and to be strengthened for the journey.

How do you find times of Sabbath rest in your life? How and when do you find Sabbath times of worship and rest if you have to work on Sundays? What do you do to make your Sabbath times meaningful?

36. O God, You Made the Sabbath Day

O God, you made the Sabbath day,
Your gift, your law, your healing way.
You also made, within each heart
A longing for this day apart.

You gave your children, long-oppressed,
Your freeing gift of Sabbath rest.
You give us Sabbath freedom, too:
Our lives are more than work we do!

Life's sacred rhythm seems long gone;
The world, unblinking, carries on.
Your Spirit calls us! Slow our pace
That we may hear your word of grace.

Christ Jesus lives! He makes us new!
On Sundays now, we worship you.
With hearts uplifted, joy restored,
Your church goes out to serve you, Lord.

Tune: TALLIS' CANON LM ("All Praise to Thee, My God, This Night"), Thomas Tallis Alternate tune: TRURO

All the Music Sung and Played Here

This hymn is often used for hymn sings and choir dedication Sundays. It celebrates the many ways of glorifying God with music, and the central role of music in the Christian faith. It also recognizes different kinds of musical gifts. See Psalms 22, 100, 148, and 150, and Luke 1:46-55.

Music has been a central part of the life of God's people for many centuries. Yet in the life of the church, music is not a performance given for the people in the congregation; it is an offering to God of the talents that God has given to people in the church. The best church choirs are the ones who really do sing for the Lord, whether the choir members are professionally trained or people who can't read music. These are people who show up at choir practice week after week because they know God loves them and they want to share their faith with others through the music of the church. Their dedicated faith is a joy in worship.

Music takes a variety of forms. Some people praise God using sign language, which has a rhythm and beauty of its own. Some people praise God by tapping their toes to the beat of a contemporary song, others by playing classical music on a pipe organ, and still others by strumming a guitar. God also calls people to offer praise who may find that their "gifts are not in singing." All of us can praise God with music in the church, whether we are singing it, playing it, listening to it, signing it, or praying it. All who know the joy of being "touched by grace" are invited to offer back God's "song of love" that God has shared with us through the centuries. In what ways do you enjoy music as part of your worship life?

See the appendix article "Why We Sing" for further reflections on this hymn.

37. All the Music Sung and Played Here

All the music sung and played here is a gift, O God, from you.
For as long as we have prayed here, we've been blessed by music, too.
By your Spirit, each musician finds new depths of faith to share.
Music is a gift you've given and becomes our thankful prayer.

All creation sings your glory; in the Psalms are pain and praise.
Mary sang your saving story in her long, expectant days.
Through the years, with great emotion, some have reached to you in song.
May we sing with such devotion; music helps your church grow strong!

You give hymns and songs for singing, toes for tapping your good news,
Organ sounding, hand bells ringing, faithful hearers in the pews.
With the trumpet and the cymbal, with guitar and violin,
Faith is found here and rekindled; hearts are lifted, once again.

Bless the talents we are bringing, for we offer you our best.
If our gifts are not in singing, may our joyful noise be blest.
If our world is ever silent, may we sign to you above.
Touched by grace, may each one present offer back your song of love.

Tune: NETTLETON 87.87 D ("Come, Thou Fount of Every Blessing"), Wyeth's *Repository of Sacred Music*, 1813

You Call Us, Lord, to Worship

This hymn celebrates the joy and importance of corporate worship. The hymn was written to the tune of a popular Easter hymn; we worship every Sunday because it is the day of our Lord's resurrection. See Acts 2:43-47 (life among the believers), Acts 20:7 and 1 Corinthians 16:2. The hymn expresses thanks for God's presence in the various parts of the order of worship as found in many churches. This is a good opening hymn for a worship service, as it celebrates what will follow.

In many churches, the order of worship lives out the story of our life of faith. We gather to praise God who is holy and good; we often begin with one or more hymns of praise. In doing so, we are reminded how we have fallen short of God's will, and so we offer a prayer of confession. The assurance of forgiveness brings us once again the good news of God's forgiving love. In response to God's peace in our lives, we share that peace with one another. We hear the good news in scripture, song, and sermon. Then we respond to that good news, with offerings, sacraments, and prayers for others. Finally we sing again as we prepare to go out and serve God for another week.

What is the most meaningful part of worship for you? What feeds you for another week? What challenges you to live differently?

38. You Call Us, Lord, to Worship

You call us, Lord, to worship; the day is set aside.
Your love is overflowing; the doors are opened wide.
Yet as we see your goodness, we see what we have been.
And so we humbly ask you, "Forgive us of our sin!"

We are forgiven people; we know your love's embrace.
The peace of Christ is with us; forgiveness fills this place.
We hear your word in scripture, in sermon and in song.
Again, again, you tell us: we're loved and we belong.

We share our joys and sorrows and then we offer prayer
For people who are hurting, for nations everywhere.
We bring our tithes and offerings, returning what is yours,
For what we keep may vanish, but what we give endures.

We celebrate your love, Lord, with water, wine and bread.
For at your font we're welcomed and at your feast we're fed.
We pray the prayer you taught us; we sing your praise and then
Through daily, faithful living, we worship you again.

Tune: LANCASHIRE 76.76 D ("The Day of Resurrection!"), Henry Thomas Smart, 1835

We Enter Your Church

Baptism is one of the great joys in the life of the church, as well as in the life of the individual Christian. This hymn emphasizes God's role in the sacrament; it reaffirms that the gift of baptism calls for a response of faithful and joyful living. See Matthew 28:16-20, 1 Corinthians 12:13, and Romans 6:4-11.

One of the greatest gifts that God gives us, in and through the church, is a sense of belonging to God. God says, "You're mine!" The church is a place of welcome, where we experience the unconditional love of God and the hospitality of God's people.

We live in a world that often puts conditions on love. "You belong with us if you think this, or act this way, or do this, or wear the right clothes, or agree with my beliefs." God simply says, "My child!" What a wonderful gift!

39. We Enter Your Church

We enter your church, Lord, through welcoming doors.
We enter it, too, where you claim us as yours.
It's here at the font that you offer a sign:
You tell us, "My children, you're baptized! You're mine!"

O God, you have called us, inviting us in;
You've made us your household and freed us from sin.
From youngest to oldest, we find in this place
Your waters of welcome, your family, your grace.

We've heard here your welcome and also your call;
Your Spirit inspires us to share Christ with all.
The life we receive here is life we can share;
We'll carry your message of love everywhere.

Tune: CRADLE SONG 11 11.11 11 ("Away in the Manger"), William James Kirkpatrick, 1895.

We Come to This Table

This hymn was commissioned as part of the World Communion Sunday resources prepared by the Presbyterian Peacemaking Program, and sent to all PC(USA) churches. Scripture references include Matthew 5:9 and 1 Corinthians 11:23-26.

The celebration of the Lord's Supper and our efforts at working for peace and justice are part of the same conversation for Christians. Galatians 3:28 reminds us: "There is no longer Jew or Greek, there is no longer slave or free, there is no longer male and female; for all of you are one in Christ Jesus." When we belong to Christ and share his holy meal, we belong to one another as brothers and sisters in Christ.

One of the most profound, moving communion services I have experienced was on the island of La Gonâve, Haiti, when I was in college. A group of students and our professor had been living and working on the island for a week. On Sunday morning, we packed into the tiny church with countless children, women and men to join in worship—and we came forward to the table to celebrate the Lord's Supper.

We came from two very different cultures, and I was very much aware of the wealth and privilege that was waiting for some of us back in the United States, as well as the ongoing hunger and poverty that surrounded the families of La Gonâve. Yet Christ made us one at that table. I also remember what happened a couple of days later, after we left that table. We were preparing to get back in the boat and leave the island when a young mother tried to give us her child. She loved her little girl so much that she was willing to never see her again, to give her a chance to survive.

I often wonder what happened to that little girl. Did she survive, and does she have children of her own now? What is our responsibility as Christians who share the table of the Lord to serve one another? What is my responsibility and yours to care for children like that little girl? How did her presence at the Lord's Table that day change my life and make me a different person? Do we "rise from the table with new dedication" to serve God? How is God calling us to serve? ❦

40. We Come to This Table

We come to this table, O God, with thanksgiving.
We lift up our hearts, we remember, we pray.
We hear Jesus' welcome—inviting, forgiving;
We know your Spirit's peace as we feast here today.

We dine at your table as sisters and brothers,
Diverse in our cultures, yet nourished as one.
The bread and the cup that we share here with others
Are gifts uniting all who are claimed by your Son.

We grieve for your world here; we cry, "How much longer?"
We pray for the cycles of violence to cease.
Yet here, in Christ broken, we're fed and made stronger
To labor in his name for a world filled with peace.

We rise from this table with new dedication
To feed the world's children, to free the oppressed,
To clear out the minefields, to care for creation;
We pray, O God of peace, that our work will be blest.

Tune: KREMSER 12 11.12 11 ("We Gather Together"), *Nederlandtsch Gedenckclanck*, 1626

There Are Many Ways of Sharing

This hymn, which is based on 1 Corinthians 12, celebrates the gifts of the Spirit for ministry. It was originally written for services of ordination and installation for Elders, Deacons and Ministers of the Word and Sacrament. It could also be used in worship services recognizing volunteers in the church or in the community, or celebrating the gifts and daily vocations of church members.

Summer is a time when many churches recruit their church school volunteers for the fall. Is every teacher planning to return to the classroom in September? If not, who could we ask to serve? When fall comes, nominating committees ask the question: Who will serve in key church leadership positions for the coming year?

Many congregations put a lot of time and effort into leadership recruitment and training; it seems that we always need more workers in the church. At the same time, we need to pause and say "thank you" to God for the variety of leaders we already have. What would the church be like if all its members were church school teachers? Or volunteers in the church office? Or youth leaders? Or stewardship committee members? Or ordained ministers? There are times when we are looking for individuals with specific gifts to get particular jobs done. Yet at the same time, we know that one of the joys of the church is this: "There are a variety of gifts" (1 Corinthians 12:4) and many people are already serving in wonderful ways.

We also know that it is the "same Spirit" who gives the gifts that the church needs. One thing that is unique about the church is that we call people "volunteers" just like many other community groups do, but we have a different awareness of how people come to us to serve. We recognize that the gifts each one brings to the church come from God— and God calls us to use them for the good of all. The initiative comes from God, who gives us abilities, seeks us out, nudges our consciences, helps us to see the need, and uses a nominating committee or a search committee to ask us to help. We are not strictly volunteers. We are people who have received gifts from God, and we have been called and challenged to use them.

Everyone who is baptized in the church is given a job to do. Everyone! Some are recognized as having leadership abilities, and they are called to be elders, deacons, or pastors, committee chairs or church school teachers. In leadership as well as in other kinds of Christian service, faith informs what we do; God's love is to be shared. So we pray, "Bless each baptized one's vocation; give each one a servant's heart."

41. There Are Many Ways of Sharing

There are many ways of sharing, But God's Spirit gives each one.
There are different ways of caring; It's one Lord whose work is done.
God, whose gifts are overflowing, May we hear you when you call;
Keep us serving, keep us growing, For the common good of all.

We've been baptized in the waters! We've been given work to do.
When you call your sons and daughters, You give gifts for serving you.
God, we join in celebration Of the talents you impart.
Bless each baptized one's vocation; Give each one a servant's heart.

All are blest by gifts you give us; Some are set apart to lead.
Give us Jesus' love within us As we care for those in need.
Give us faith to make decisions; Give us joy to share your Word.
Give us unity and vision As we serve your church and world.

Tune: NETTLETON 87.87 D ("Come, Thou Fount of Every Blessing"), Wyeth's *Repository of Sacred Music*, 1813

Alternate Tune: ABBOT'S LEIGH

O God, We Rage at Hurtful Things

This hymn was inspired by a friend who emailed asking for prayers for a young child in her church who was critically ill. It has been used in services of wholeness and healing—services that are found in increasing numbers across the Church. The Psalms are filled with both lament and trust; see Psalms 6, 22, 23, 31:10, 38, and 102. See also John 9:1-12.

The Letter of James 5:14-15 instructs us to anoint and pray for those who are ill: "Are any among you sick? They should call for the elders of the church and have them pray over them, anointing them with oil in the name of the Lord. The prayer of faith will save the sick, and the Lord will raise them up; and anyone who has committed sins will be forgiven." From the beginning, the church has followed Jesus' example and cared for the sick.

One of the ways that we care for people is by praying for them, yet sometimes our prayers are filled with anguish and anger, more than with hope and trust. Sometimes we want to cry out, "It's just not fair!" The Psalms—those wonderful prayers that have challenged and comforted so many people of faith—show us that it is all right for us to be angry with God when we suffer. We can shout out, "Why, Lord? Why?" Many of those laments in the Psalms also gently lead us in a new direction, because they end with words of trust. We find comfort in God's loving care even in times of pain and loss.

As Christians, we pray for healing, that comes in many forms. We also pray simply that when the journey seems too rough, it will be enough that God is with us. When have you needed to know healing, in your own life, or in the life of someone you love? Have you found an answer to that prayer? What was the answer?

42. O God, We Rage at Hurtful Things

O God, we rage at hurtful things
Beyond our own control,
Like all the pain that illness brings
To body, mind and soul.

There's much we cannot understand;
O Lord, we ask you, "Why?"
And yet in Christ you know firsthand
The tears your people cry.

O Christ, your loving, saving touch
Heals children, women, men.
We pray for ones we love so much;
Lord, make them whole again.

Now work through those your Spirit sends
To heal, restore and care.
May doctors, nurses, neighbors, friends
Be answers to our prayer.

And when the journey seems too rough
And you seem far away,
Remind us, Lord: You are enough
To bring us through each day.

Tune: St. Anne CM ("Our God, Our Help in Ages Past"), attr. William Croft, 1708

God, Your Love and Care Surround Us

This is a revised funeral hymn, based on another hymn that appeared in my earlier book, *Gifts of Love: New Hymns for Today's Worship*. The words and tune have been changed a bit, but the theme of the hymn continues to be God's love that leads us into eternal life. See Revelation 21:5; John 14:1-6 and Revelation 21:1-4.

Did you ever skip rocks or toss pebbles into the still water of a quiet pond? The tiniest splash can make circles of water that go out and meet other circles of water from other pebbles. Our lives are like those pebbles, and our relationships are like those rings of water. God created us so that our lives touch the lives of other people around us, allowing them to make a difference in our lives, too.

The many relationships we have with others can be good ones or they can be troubling. Sometimes death comes unexpectedly to someone we love; it may come before we have a chance to work things out with the person, when feelings have been hurt or someone has been wronged. Sometimes, the other person may have refused to change, leaving us feeling that there is no closure for a bad situation. So we pray, "Help us, in our joy, remember; help us, in our pain, forgive."

Whatever else death may bring, it brings the end of a relationship for now. Yet we find hope in Jesus' words, "In my Father's house there are many dwelling places" (John 14:2). We look forward to a time when "God will wipe every tear from [our] eyes" (Revelation 21:1-4). We know God's presence in the valley of the shadow of death.

At other times in our lives, we may focus on things that seem to be overwhelmingly important—finances, work, vacation plans, church challenges and conflicts. At times of loss, we are reminded of what really matters—our relationship with God and our relationship with others.

43. God, Your Love and Care Surround Us

God, your love and care surround us every moment, every day.
Now we gather to remember one who followed Jesus' way.
Grateful for this life you've given, now we give it back to you,
Trusting your eternal promise: "I am making all things new!"

As an ordinary pebble tossed upon a quiet pond
Sends out rings of rippling waters, moving waters far beyond—
So we touch the lives of others; We are moved by how they live.
Help us, in our joy, remember; help us, in our pain, forgive.

"Do not let your hearts be troubled," Jesus said to those he loved.
"There are many dwelling places in my Father's house above."
Jesus, you have gone before us; Jesus, you will guide us there.
Lord, we trust your hand to lead us to the place that you prepare.

We hold onto what you promise: Earth and heav'n will be made new.
Then your home will be among us; we will always dwell with you.
There will be no sound of weeping; you will wipe away each tear.
God, we trust your promise to us: Now and always, you are here.

Tune: BEECHER 87.87 D ("Love Divine, All Loves Excelling"), John Zundel, 1870
Text: Copyright © 2002 by Carolyn Winfrey Gillette. All rights reserved.

O God Whose Loving Has No End

This hymn was written after the tragic death of David MacKnight from a heart attack. He was the loving husband of our church secretary, loving and caring father of two children, and a gifted musician. The tune seems appropriate because of his Scottish heritage (bagpipes were played at his service). See John 14:1-6, Revelation 7:17 and 21:4.

When anyone we love dies, there is a lot of grief. When a young person dies, we grieve not only the loss of the person, but also the loss of what might have been—the moments never shared, the music never sung. Times of death remind us that we need and depend on God's gifts of faith, hope and love. We wait for the day described in Revelation 21, when God will wipe away every tear from our eye. In the meantime, we thank God for gifts of comfort: "For faith that leads us through, For hope that patiently uplifts, For love that makes us new."

In what ways have you mourned the loss of what might have been, when someone died? How have faith, hope and love been healing gifts in your life?

44. O God Whose Loving Has No End

O God whose loving has no end,
We grieve for one who died:
We mourn a husband, father, friend*
No longer at our side.

We grieve for moments never shared,
For music never sung.
Yet we have hope! Our Christ prepared
For us a glorious home.

We thank you, Lord, for healing gifts:
For faith that leads us through,
For hope that patiently uplifts,
For love that makes us new.

O help us, Lord, to wait the day
That we cannot yet see,
When you'll wipe every tear away
For all eternity.

*Alternate wording:
"We mourn a mother, wife and friend"
"We mourn a woman, neighbor, friend"
or similar line

Tune: CRIMOND CM ("The Lord's My Shepherd, I'll Not Want"), Jessie Seymour Irvine, 1872.
Text: Copyright © 2002 by Carolyn Winfrey Gillette. All rights reserved.

Go Walk with God

This hymn is one way of saying good-bye in the context of worship. It was written when my husband Bruce and I were saying good-bye to the First Presbyterian Church in Pitman, New Jersey, a congregation that we had served as co-pastors for ten years. The middle verse is based on the words of the Trinitarian blessing that many ministers use for a benediction each Sunday, the words of 2 Corinthians 13:13: "The grace of the Lord Jesus Christ, the love of God, and the communion of the Holy Spirit be with all of you." The hymn ends with an acknowledgement from I Corinthians 13:8 that is the source of our hope, even as we say good-bye to people we care about: Love never ends. This hymn can be used as a Benediction response on any Sunday as well as at times when church members who are leaving the community are recognized.

Several years ago, our son John left home for his freshman year of college. We are proud of the young man he has become, which made it a little easier to send him off with our prayers and with a sense of confidence that he would do well in college and in life. As he left for his freshman year, we knew that we would miss him. We looked forward to holidays, summer breaks, and other times when we would be together again as a family.

We were reminded then, as we are now, that our lives are filled with transitions and changes. An elderly widow sorts through her possessions, packs up the most important ones and moves to a retirement home closer to her children, a hundred miles from her friends and church community. A father or mother receives a job transfer, and the family moves in the middle of the school year to a new community. These are occasions to say "good-bye," an expression which originally meant "God be with you."

Family, friendships, and a church community are central to many of our lives. Yet we live in a culture that is transient, and every year, there are times when we need to acknowledge that someone we care about is going away.

When have you said good-bye this year? What was the occasion? How can we say good-bye in the context of a faith community? Does your church include good-byes in worship and fellowship times? In what ways? How do the words "love never ends" bring hope to you?

45. Go Walk with God

Go walk with God in all you do,
And may God's love bring joy to you.
May gifts of peace fill all your days,
And may God's truth guide you always.

O may the grace of Christ our Lord,
The wondrous love that comes from God,
The Spirit's fellowship now be
God's gifts to you eternally.

We thank you, Lord, for life we share
In learning, serving, praise and prayer.
And when we say good-bye to friends,
We thank you, Lord: Love never ends.

Tune: O WALY WALY LM ("Though I May Speak"), English folk melody.
Alternate Tune: TALLIS CANON
Text: Copyright © 2004 by Carolyn Winfrey Gillette. All rights reserved.

Church Celebrations

You've Called Us Together, O God, by Your Grace

This hymn was commissioned by the Executive Committee of the Consultation on Church Union to celebrate the creation of a new organization, Churches Uniting in Christ. This organization seeks to strengthen the ties between the African Methodist Episcopal Church, African Methodist Episcopal Zion Church, Christian Church (Disciples of Christ), Christian Methodist Episcopal Church, Episcopal Church, International Council of Community Churches, Moravian Church Northern Province, Presbyterian Church (USA), United Church of Christ, and United Methodist Church. "You've Called Us Together" was first sung at the Inaugural Celebration of Churches Uniting in Christ on January 20, 2002 in Memphis, Tennessee; it has been sung at many ecumenical gatherings, at congregational worship services and at the PC(USA) General Assembly.

Ephesians 4:4-6 reminds us: "There is one body and one Spirit, just as you were called to the one hope of your calling, one Lord, one faith, one baptism, one God and Father of all, who is above all and through all and in all." In John's gospel, we find Jesus' prayer, "The glory that you have given me I have given them, so that they may be one, as we are one, I in them and you in me, that they may become completely one, so that the world may know that you have sent me . . . " (John 17:22-23).

Whenever Christians bicker among themselves, when one denomination denies the faithfulness of another, when Christians refuse to work with each other on mission projects because of doctrinal disputes, there is sadness in the Church. I am reminded of the words of an old, traditional hymn, "The Church's One Foundation": "Though with a scornful wonder This world sees her oppressed, By schisms rent asunder, By heresies distressed, Yet saints their watch are keeping; Their cry goes up: 'How long?' " We wait for the time when the "night of weeping shall be the morn of song."

In the meantime, there are signs of grace in the Church. In the last three years, we have hosted Catholic and Protestant youth from Northern Ireland at our church who were here for a month-long program together. We have seen conservative Christians and liberal Christians travel on mission trips together. We have shared in ecumenical worship services at Thanksgiving, during Advent and on Good Friday. We have worked with Christians of many backgrounds to care for children in need. And we have been reminded, with many other Christians:

> "Our new common mission has only begun;
> We're learning the blessings of serving as one."

46. You've Called Us Together, O God, by Your Grace

You've called us together, O God, by your grace;
In grateful obedience, we've come to this place.
Our new common mission has only begun;
We're learning the blessings of serving as one.

Refrain:
We are called! We are freed!
We are baptized as one.
In the Church, all we need
Can be found in your Son!
With Christ to unite us, and born from above,
We witness together to your wondrous love.

We're one in the faith, and in creeds that we share,
In worship and sacraments, scripture and prayer.
We're one in our seeking to follow Christ's way,
In Spirit-led ministry, day after day.

Refrain

There's much to rejoice in, yet much to be done;
While some are excluded, we can't live as one.
May we as your churches uniting now see
That justice is needed for true unity.

Refrain

Tune: To God Be The Glory 11 11.11 11 with refrain, William Howard Doane, 1875.
Text: Copyright © 2001 by Carolyn Winfrey Gillette. All rights reserved.

We Look to You, O Jesus

This hymn was commissioned for the 300th anniversary celebration of American Presbyterians on October 1, 2006, held at Old Pine Street Presbyterian Church in Philadelphia. It is based on the words of Hebrews 12:2: " . . . looking to Jesus the pioneer and perfecter of our faith, who for the sake of the joy that was set before him endured the cross, disregarding its shame, and has taken his seat at the right hand of the throne of God."

Did you ever stop and think about how your community and the world have changed in the last three hundred years? As we celebrate special anniversaries in the church, it is good to learn a bit of history—and not just about wars, battles and presidents. What were our ancestors like? What did they experience in their everyday lives? What was it like to be part of a church, a century or more ago?

My great-grandfather was a Baptist preacher who received part of his pay in chickens, eggs, and produce from parishioners. My parents told me that there used to be a tradition known as "pounding the preacher," where every family in the church would bring in a pound of something—flour, corn, vegetables, etc.—for the minister's family. I am grateful to have a regular salary from the church where we serve! Yet I continue to wonder about my great-grandfather's life and ministry. I treasure a small, bound, brown-on-the-edges appointment book that he carried with him as he made his rounds; it is a far cry from the computer I often use. My great-grandfather lived in a time and culture I have trouble imagining. Yet his faith and mine have so much in common, and he is part of the great cloud of witnesses cheering us on, on our journey.

In looking at our history, we look not only at people a few generations back. We look at the "big picture" of salvation history. God created everything and called it good. God sent the prophets to call us back when we wondered away. God sent Jesus Christ his Son, the pioneer of our faith, and the perfecter as well. ❧

47. We Look to You, O Jesus

We look to you, O Jesus—in faith, our Pioneer—
For you have gone before us and brought your people here.
You showed us all God's kingdom, you gave us work to do;
In death you went before us; for life, we turn to you.

We looked to you to guide us three hundred years ago;
How different was the land then, from this land that we know.
With towns and country growing, your people heard your call,
And so they built new churches, proclaiming you to all.

Through times of strife and anguish, through times of joy and grace,
Through conflicts with our culture, you've brought us to this place;
And still your world is changing, and still we seek to be
A church reformed, reforming in faithful ministry.

Perfecter of the faith, Lord, we look to you each day;
We work for peace and justice, we worship, learn and pray—
And witnesses surround us, a host of saints above,
As we continue sharing the joy of your great love.

Tune: LANCASHIRE 76.76 D ("The Day of Resurrection!"), Henry Thomas Smart, 1835

Looking Back, O God, We Wonder

Ralph and Anita Johnson requested this hymn for their beloved congregation, New Castle Presbyterian Church in New Castle, Delaware, where Ralph served as pastor for many years. The church was celebrating its 350th anniversary. See Matthew 25:38-40, which is the basis for the third verse.

Whenever a church celebrates an anniversary, there are plenty of opportunities to look back at what has gone before. Use your imagination and think about the people who are part of your church's history. What were they like? What children have played, and what adults have worked in the shadow of your church building? Does your church have "well-worn pews"? If so, who sat in them for generations before you? What did they pray for? What did the church building look like years ago? How has it changed?

Look at your church today. Who are your brothers and sisters in Christ in the church pews? How does your church welcome new people? How do you see the face of Christ in each one? How do you serve your community and your world?

Look at where your church is going. What do you wonder about the future? Where is God leading your congregation?

48. Looking Back, O God, We Wonder

Looking back, O God, we wonder of that time in history
When the early settlers gathered, building this community.
Children did their chores and played here; men and women worked the land.
Sundays, Lord, they knelt and prayed here, seeking your protecting hand.

Looking to your love, we worship as your people long have done,
Sharing bread and Word and friendship, singing praises to your Son.
Bricks of old are such a treasure, well-worn pews proclaim our past;
But your love beyond all measure is the treasure that will last.

Looking out, we see our neighbors, and—in each one—Jesus' face.
God, we offer you our labors so that all will know your grace.
As we witness all around us, as we welcome strangers in,
As we help those lost and homeless, your church welcomes you again.

Looking on to where we're going, God, we wonder what will be;
Yet we trust your Spirit, knowing you will guide our ministry.
You give each new generation ways to praise you, work to do;
God, be with this congregation as we keep on serving you.

Tune: HYMN TO JOY 87.87 D ("Joyful, Joyful, We Adore Thee"), Ludwig van Beethoven, 1824
Text: Copyright © 2006 by Carolyn Winfrey Gillette. All rights reserved.

God, We Join in Celebration

The historic Neshaminy-Warwick Presbyterian Church commissioned this hymn to celebrate the church's 275th anniversary. For this hymn, see Matthew 5:13-14 and 13:33, as well as 28:16-20.

Since this hymn was written for one particular congregation's anniversary celebration, the original text included this opening verse rather than the more inclusive verse below:

> God, we join in celebration of your love and faithfulness:
> Long ago, our congregation gathered in the wilderness.
> In those days, the first Log College, here by the Neshaminy,
> Offered youth the gift of knowledge and your truth that set them free.

In the very end of Matthew's gospel, we find the words of Jesus' "Great Commission" to his disciples: "All authority in heaven and on earth has been given to me. Go therefore and make disciples of all nations, baptizing them in the name of the Father and of the Son and of the Holy Spirit, and teaching them to obey everything that I have commanded you. And remember, I am with you always, to the end of the age" (Matthew 28:18-20). How does the Great Commission guide your church? How do you answer God's call for you to love your neighbors? Early in Matthew's gospel, Jesus says, "You are the salt of the earth . . . You are the light of the world" (Matthew 13:33). He also taught, "The kingdom of heaven is like yeast that a woman took and mixed in with three measures of flour until all of it was leavened" (Matthew 13:33). How is your congregation salt and light and leaven in a changing world? 🌱

49. God, We Join in Celebration

God, we join in celebration of your love and faithfulness:
Long ago, our congregation gathered in the wilderness.
Long ago, your people worshiped, shared the gospel, served you well,
Celebrated grace and friendship, then went out, your love to tell.

What a faith-filled, rich tradition we are blest, O Christ, to know.
Guided by your Great Commission, many helped our church to grow.
Called by you to love their neighbors, thousands served you here with grace.
Thank you for their loving labors that have brought us to this place.

Grateful for the past you've given, now we look in hope to you.
Make us salt, and light, and leaven, working for a world that's new.
By your Spirit, lead and guide us as your loving family,
Teach us, shape us, walk beside us! Send us out in ministry!

Tune: HYMN TO JOY 87.87 D ("Joyful, Joyful, We Adore Thee"), Ludwig van Beethoven, 1824

God, When You Called Our Church by Grace

This hymn was commissioned by pastor Dave Davis to celebrate the 250th anniversary of the Blackwood Presbyterian Church in Blackwood, New Jersey. The tune reflects the congregation's love of old gospel hymns. Scripture references include: Matthew 21:42, Mark 12:10, Luke 20:17, Acts 4:11, Ephesians 2:20 and 1 Peter 2:6.

Does your church have a cornerstone? Is there some place on the outside of your church building that reminds you about the time when your church was built? Think about what promise your church building held for those Christians who first worshiped in it.

We know that a church is more than a collection of building materials put together in the right configuration. Our true cornerstone is not a piece of granite but Jesus Christ. And our best promises don't come from what a building can offer, but from God working in and through us. With God's help, we can all be a faithful, loving, serving church. How has God kept his promises to be with and to guide your church?

50. God, When You Called Our Church by Grace

God, when you called our church by grace,
This land was such a different place.
Yet what you spoke remains the same:
"I'll be with you! Go in my name!"

Your promise is for everyone:
You call us here; your word is true!
We'll be a faithful church for you!

Lord Jesus Christ, our cornerstone,
You meet us here; we're not alone!
Through times of joy, through tears long-wept,
You are God's love, God's promise kept.

Your promise is for everyone:
You love us all, you make us new!
We'll be a loving church for you!

O Holy Spirit, wind and flame,
You send us out in Jesus' name.
You give us gifts that we may share
God's love and justice everywhere.

Your promise is for everyone:
You give us gifts, and work to do!
We'll be a serving church for you!

Tune: THE SOLID ROCK LM with refrain ("My Hope Is Built on Nothing Less"), William Batchelder
Bradbury, 1863
Text: Copyright © 2000 by Carolyn Winfrey Gillette. All rights reserved.

When We Were a Younger Nation

This hymn celebrates the 175th anniversary of First Presbyterian Church, Allentown, Pennsylvania. Gloria S. Snyder, the church's Director of Music Administration and Organist, commissioned the hymn.

When we moved to Wilmington, Delaware, we found ourselves living in a much more culturally diverse community. This has given our teenage children wonderful opportunities to make new friends from a variety of cultures, religious traditions, and family backgrounds.

One time, our younger daughter Sarah was invited to a birthday party. Unlike many other birthday parties among her group of friends, it would not be a sleepover party. The teenager celebrating her birthday was Muslim, and she couldn't have the sleepover from Friday night to Saturday because of her family's holy day; yet she said she would not have a sleepover party from Saturday night to Sunday either. She appreciated that her friends respected her faith, and she wanted to respect their Christian faith, so she did not want to interfere with Sunday, the holy day of her Christian friends. The party was simply held on Saturday evening and all the girls went home that night. Another time, this same group of lunch table friends—Muslim, Jewish and Christian—together attended the Bat Mitvah of a Jewish friend.

While we treasure the wonderful life we receive in Jesus Christ, we are grateful that our children are growing up in a world where teenagers from diverse backgrounds can be friends. We live in an ever-changing nation, and God has indeed shown us how we can welcome others in.

The Allentown Church, for which this hymn was written, has some wonderful programs and ministries that encourage dialogue between various religious and cultural groups in their community. Does your congregation have opportunities to reach out in hospitality and conversation with others? Do you, as an individual?

51. When We Were a Younger Nation

When we were a younger nation,
When new settlers filled this land—
God, you called this congregation
By your guiding, caring hand.
Those you gathered shared a language
And a life of love and praise;
Through your grace, they spread your message
In those pioneering days.

We, your church, have seen great wonders
As we've known Christ's presence here.
We have welcomed in new members;
We've been blessed from year to year.
Through our music and our worship,
Through our teaching of your word,
Through our laughter and our friendship,
We've proclaimed it: "God is good!"

Yet your goodness that we cherish
Can't be kept within this place;
So you send us out in service,
Doing justice, seeking peace.
Spirit-filled, we heal the broken,
Build new houses—new lives, too;
God, in ways both lived and spoken,
We have sought to follow you.

In an ever-changing nation,
God, you call us yet again;
You have shown this generation
How to welcome others in.
Crossings bounds of faith and culture,
May we learn and grow and share;
And may we, your church, be faithful,
Loving, serving everywhere.

Tune: RUSTINGTON 87.87.D ("Out of Deep, Unordered Water"), C. Hubert H. Parry, 1897
Alternate tune: BEACH SPRING
Text: Copyright © 2006 by Carolyn Winfrey Gillette. All rights reserved.

How Lovely Is Your Church, O Lord!

This hymn was written for worship at an annual regional meeting built around the theme of service. The meeting was held in an old, historic church called St. Anne's (hence the tune), which was also celebrating an anniversary The hymn makes reference to Psalm 84:1, 10 and Jeremiah 1:4-8.

For many of us who grew up in it, the church is a wonderful home away from home. In fact, for some people, it is the best home they have ever known. At its best, the church is a place of welcome, love and community in a world that can be harsh and uncaring at times. It's a place where we learn God's grace, where we discover with joy that Christ served us, where we are challenged by Christ's call to serve one another and to serve the poor.

This hymn begins with an allusion to Psalm 84 and ends with our own service that reflects Christ's love. How have you expressed your thanks for your church today? How has God called your church to ministries of caring for those in need?

52. How Lovely Is Your Church, O Lord!

How lovely is your church, O Lord,
Where we can sing and pray;
One day within your courts is more
Than thousands far away.

Within these walls we come to know
Your grace, so undeserved!
For at the table Christ knelt low
To be the one who served.

You give your Spirit's blessings here
Then send us from this place
To challenge hatred, greed, and fear
With gifts of love and grace.

At times we're filled with troubling doubt:
"I'm old!" "I'm young!" "I'm weak!"
Yet you who sent the prophets out
Will give us words to speak.

How lovely is your church, O Lord,
When we are serving you!
For when we serve the lost and poor,
Your love is shining through.

Tune: ST. ANNE CM ("Our God, Our Help in Ages Past"), attr. William Croft, 1708
Text: Copyright © 2005 by Carolyn Winfrey Gillette. All rights reserved.

God of Love, We Sing Your Glory

Every church has a story. Some congregations' stories go back hundreds of years, and some are much shorter. This hymn was written for the church we are serving now as co-pastors, Limestone Presbyterian Church, when they were celebrating their fiftieth anniversary. See Matthew 5:14-16, 1 Corinthians 12, 2 Corinthians 5:17, and Hebrews 11:1.

Limestone Church is typical of many churches begun in the 1950s: It was started as a mission outreach in an area where farms were turning into suburbs. It is a church that cares deeply about mission work and wants to reach out to help others in the community and around the world.

Every church, old or new, needs to find its way in a changing world; what has worked in the past may not work today. Yet old ways need to be honored, even as church members and leaders try new things.

How does a church grow? Guided by the Holy Spirit, how does any church change in form or priorities in order to be more faithful to God? We can never be the church on our own; how does God's Spirit guide us in ministry?

53. God of Love, We Sing Your Glory

God of love, we sing your glory and we offer you our praise,
As we celebrate the story of our church's founding days.
'Mid the farms and homes around here, faithful Christians heard your call:
"This is truly mission ground here; be my light that shines to all."

From the start, we were a mission, sent to share Christ's love and grace.
Through the years, we've kept that vision as we've served you in this place.
As we've sought to be a blessing to the lonely, lost and poor,
What we've found has been surprising: you have blessed us even more.

When we gather here to worship, still your blessings overflow.
Education, faith and friendship are your gifts through which we grow.
Called to serve, we seek a balance: honor old ways, try what's new!
Spirit-filled, we share our talents and are blessed by serving you.

God, we pray about the future, and we wonder what will be;
Yet we know it's an adventure joining hands in ministry.
For in church, each generation builds by faith and not by sight—
And each one, a new creation, finds new ways to spread your light.

Tune: NETTLETON 87.87 D ("Come, Thou Fount of Every Blessing"), Wyeth's *Repository of Sacred Music*, 1813
Text: Copyright © 2006 by Carolyn Winfrey Gillette. All rights reserved.

God, We Have Come from Our Families and Homes

This hymn was written to celebrate the thirtieth anniversary of Ulster Project Delaware. For three summers, our Limestone congregation along with a Roman Catholic parish co-sponsored and hosted twenty-five Catholic and Protestant youth from Northern Ireland for a month. Through a variety of shared events, from sightseeing to service projects, the youth overcame barriers and grew in respect for one another. This hymn was commissioned to celebrate the peacemaking work that has taken place over three decades. It was a joy to be with the Irish youth when they got the news that the Irish Republican Army had finally agreed to disarm. The hymn has been sung not only in the United States but also in Ireland. See John 17:20-23.

When we think about Jesus' prayer, we usually think about the Lord's Prayer, "Our Father, who art in heaven . . ." In John 17, there is another, much longer prayer in which our Lord prays for unity among the people who would follow him. Take some time to read this prayer. First, read it straight through. Then read it slowly and carefully, a verse or two at a time. Meditate on the words. Listen for how Jesus was praying for you.

So many denominations and congregations are going through times of conflict. What does Jesus' prayer have to say to us as we seek to build bridges of reconciliation? When have you had the opportunity to work with other Christians in a situation where you gathered as strangers and left as friends?

54. God, We Have Come from Our Families and Homes

God, we have come from our families and homes,
Seeking the things that will make us all one.
For we know now—the things that divide
And how divisions have hurt us inside.

You sent us Jesus, who prayed for his own:
"Make them all one so your love will be known."
Making new friends—may we understand
We are love's bearers throughout every land.

Great strength and might will not bring us success—
Yet by your Spirit our lives will be blest!
Give us new dreams—of what life can be;
Help us to work for a new harmony.

Lord, as we worship and sightsee and play,
And as we listen to what others say,
Days turn to weeks—until this time ends;
Gathered as strangers, may we leave as friends.

Tune: SLANE 10.10.9.10 ("Be Thou My Vision"), Irish Ballad.

Lord, What a Cloud of Witnesses

My husband and co-pastor Bruce requested that I write this hymn after he was asked to lead worship for a meeting of the Board of Directors of the Presbyterian Historical Society. Many congregations have used this hymn as part of their anniversary celebrations. Scripture references include: Hebrews 11-12:1, Joshua 24:13, and John 14:26.

Over the years, we have sat in bleachers watching the soccer games of our children, John, Catherine, and Sarah. We have cheered them on in their victories and worried when someone got hurt. As a family, we have also enjoyed seeing some professional baseball and soccer games. Whether there are just a few people watching a local kids' game or thousands watching professional athletes play, it is fun to see the excitement and enthusiasm of a crowd cheering on those players.

This is the wonderful image of Hebrews 12: "Therefore, since we are surrounded by so great a cloud of witnesses, let us also lay aside every weight and the sin that clings so closely, and let us run with perseverance the race that is set before us . . . "

Who are the witnesses who came before you, who inspired you in your faith? In what way do they continue to be an important part of your faith and life, even if they are no longer with you physically? How is your faith built on the faith of those who came before you? How do you live in towns that others made, and harvest what you did not sow?

55. Lord, What a Cloud of Witnesses!

Lord, what a cloud of witnesses
Surrounds us as we work and pray!
Their faithful, loving service is
An inspiration every day.

We live in towns that others made;
We harvest what we did not sow—
And others sweated, labored, prayed
To build Christ's church in which we grow.

Your Spirit gives us memory;
Now give your church clear vision, too.
Reformed, reforming, may we be
A church that seeks to follow you.

Tune: TRURO LM ("Lift Up Your Heads, Ye Mighty Gates"), *Psalmodia Evangelica*, 1789.
Alternate Tune: TALLIS' CANON
Text: Copyright © 2000 by Carolyn Winfrey Gillette. All rights reserved.

The Church in the World

In Times of Great Decision

This hymn was inspired by the National Council of Churches' "Christian Principles at the Time of an Election." It got wide use in the year 2004 and has continued to be popular, not only during secular elections, but also for congregational meetings. It appeared in *Christian Century* magazine. Biblical references include Micah 6:6-8; Amos 5:21-24; Matthew 7:7-12; Mark 12:28-34; Isaiah 65:17-25; Hebrews 13:1-9a, 16; and Psalm 104.

Since we believe that Jesus Christ is Lord, this means that we trust that he is in charge of all areas of our lives—personal, family, church, social, community, nation and world. Our faith will influence our politics and, yes, the way we vote.

This doesn't mean that Christians are only concerned about one voting issue or another. Broad principles of faith can guide us "in times of great decision." We can ask: Are these leaders concerned about peace, justice, community-building, working globally, welcoming the stranger, caring for "the least of these," and caring for creation? The Bible tells us these things are important. How do these values help us decide who our leaders should be?

56. In Times of Great Decision

In times of great decision, Be with us, God, we pray!
Give each of us a vision Of Jesus' loving way.
When louder words seem endless And other voices sure,
Remind us of your promise: Your love and truth endure.
O God, whose gifts are countless, You send us bearing peace.
You fill our dreams with justice For all communities.
You give us global neighbors, That all may justly live.
May those we choose as leaders Reflect the life you give.
O God, you bridged the distance; You opened wide your door.
You call us by our presence To reach to serve the poor.
You teach us: Welcome strangers! Seek justice on the earth!
May those we choose as leaders See every person's worth.
You call on every nation To put aside all greed,
To care for your creation And for your ones in need,
To care for those in prison, For children, for the ill.
In times of great decision, may we choose leaders well.

Tune: AURELIA 76.76 D ("The Church's One Foundation"), Samuel Sebastian Wesley, 1864.
Alternate Tune: LLANGLOFFAN

O God of Life, Your Healing Touch

This hymn was commissioned by Baylor University's Center for Christian Ethics for a travel and worship journal for a medical mission team. It was written to a tune by David Bolin which can be found at www3.baylor.edu/christianethics/hymnGillette.pdf. It can also be sung to St. Columba ("The King of Love My Shepherd Is"), which makes it a hymn of eight shorter verses instead of four longer ones. If it is used in a service of healing and wholeness, it might be divided into two or four parts, and interspersed with scripture readings, or placed throughout the homily or sermon.

The gospels are filled with stories of Jesus healing people. Mark's gospel begins with a wonderful collection of healing stories in the first three chapters alone: Jesus healed the man with an unclean spirit (1:21-28), many people at Simon's house (1:29-34), someone with leprosy (1:40-45), a person who is paralyzed (2:1-11), and a man with a "withered hand" (3:1-6). Through Jesus Christ, God certainly did "unleash gifts of healing." "New sight, new strength, and new life" are all signs of God's love and God's kingdom. The healing of the world does not end with the miracles that Jesus did so long ago. God sends us out in Jesus' name to bring physical, emotional, and spiritual healing to others. Some people have the skills to be part of a medical mission team. Others serve as volunteers in local hospitals. Others provide pastoral care to people who are sick. Still others help those who are poor in their communities to get the medical care they need. God gives us patience and strength to keep on reaching out, again and again, even when we grow tired of it. There is no "limit to our mission." We have a lifelong calling to serve.

God also sends us out to hear the truth in other people's stories, to listen to their hopes and fears, and to learn from them. Part of our maturing in the faith is to "bend a little" so that we can hear the truth of God working in other people's lives as well as in our own way of thinking and doing. How have you learned from people who have a completely different outlook on life than you do? How have those you have sought to serve brought healing to you?

57. O God of Life, Your Healing Touch

O God of life, your healing touch
Brings wholeness and salvation!
In you, this world you love so much
Becomes a new creation.

Through Jesus Christ you blessed the poor,
Unleashed your gifts of healing.
You gave new sight, new strength, new life—
To all, your love revealing.

O Christ, the loving healer still,
You gather us for mission
To serve your people who are ill,
Whatever their condition.

You send us to the suffering
With medicine and caring;
Now make our lives an offering
To those who are despairing.

Lord, by your Spirit, may we hear
The truth of others' stories.
May we respect their doubts and fears,
Their hopes and dreams, their worries.

And when their ways are not our own,
Lord, give us understanding:
Our faith cannot be fully grown
When we are too unbending.

How long, Lord, shall we serve the poor—
A week, a month, a season?
We ask the question, hoping for
A limit to our mission.

But open wide our hearts anew
And show us, as we're giving,
Your life-long call to serving you
In daily, generous living.

Tune: ST. COLUMBA ("The King of Love My Shepherd Is")
Original Tune: Kety, see www3.baylor.edu/christianethics/hymnGillette.pdf
Text: Carolyn Winfrey Gillette, 2004

God, With Joy We Look Around Us

A seminary classmate, Richard Lanford, was serving as the pastor at St. Peter's United Church of Christ in Skokie, Illinois, when the Ku Klux Klan announced they were going to have a rally in front of the Cook County Courthouse a few days before Christmas. Richard asked that a hymn be written that the churches in the community could sing to counter the hate group's rally. The hymn tune is a traditional Christmas tune, reflecting the season of year when it was first sung. The hymn has since been used by many churches as part of their annual celebrations of Martin Luther King, Jr.'s birthday.

We hope and pray that there is less prejudice than there used to be—that things are getting better—but we still see attitudes of hatred, intolerance and fear in too many places. You know where it exists in your own community. You know the work that still needs to be done. Colossians 1:19 reminds us of the meaning of Christ's coming into our world: "For in him all the fullness of God was pleased to dwell, and through him God was pleased to reconcile to himself all things, whether on earth or in heaven, by making peace through the blood of his cross." Jesus Christ is the one who tears down the walls that divide us. What walls of hatred and prejudice need to be taken down in your community? In your life?

When this hymn was first sung by churches struggling to respond to a Klan rally in their community, they had a creative response beyond the hymn. In addition to inviting people of faith to attend services in their houses of worship, they also encouraged them to pledge money for a group working to end racism, the Southern Poverty Law Center. So, even as the Klan rally was going on outside, people of faith were responding with acts of worship, peace and justice.

58. God, With Joy We Look Around Us

God, with joy we look around us
At your world's diversity.
Folk of every kind surround us
And you call your church to see:
All are made in your own image!
All are people whom you love!

In the times we've hurt each other,
Lord, we've hurt the ones you bless.
Hating sister, cursing brother,
We've denied what you express:
All are made in your own image!
All are people whom you love!

God, you sent a Savior to us,
Breaking walls that would divide.
By your Spirit, now work through us
As we witness side by side:
All are made in your own image!
All are people whom you love!

Tune: REGENT SQUARE 87.87.87 ("Angels, from the Realms of Glory"), Henry Thomas Smart, 1867
Text: Copyright © 2000 by Carolyn Winfrey Gillette. All rights reserved.

God, We Spend a Lifetime Growing

Long-time Princeton Seminary Professor of Christian Education and good friend Freda A. Gardner has taught many seminars on older adult ministry and the spirituality of "chronologically gifted" church members. This hymn was written in consultation with her. It has received wide use, due in part to its posting by the (PCUSA) Mid-Atlantic Synod's Older Adult Ministry Task Force web site.

"God, We Spend a Lifetime Growing" celebrates the gifts of older people and the ministry they offer the church and world. We learn from their faithfulness and their life experiences.

I remember one older church friend whom we used to visit when our children were small. She could no longer leave her home very often; yet in the years she was homebound, she read the entire series of *Barclay Daily Study Bible* commentaries on the New Testament. She prayed her way daily through the church's *Mission Yearbook* and she prayed for everyone in our local congregation's pictorial directory, one photo or one name at a time. She regularly made phone calls to other homebound people in the congregation, checking on them. She cared for God's creation by filling the birdfeeder outside her window. She welcomed our young children when they came with us to visit her.

Mary was a witness to all of us, as she continued to serve God in all the years she was given. This hymn reminds us, too, of God's abiding presence with us even in the challenging times, when health begins to fail: "Lord, we trust that you remember, hold us close, and see us home."

59. God, We Spend a Lifetime Growing

God, we spend a lifetime growing, learning of your love and care,
Planting seeds you give for sowing, working for the fruit they'll bear.
Now we honor faithful servants who, with joy, look back and see
Years of growing in your presence, lives of fruitful ministry.

Thank you, Lord, for ones who teach us what has brought them to this place!
May their faith-filled witness reach us; may we glimpse in them your grace.
Strong in you, their strength uplifts us from our birth until life's end;
Spirit-filled, they give us gifts, as prophet, mentor, guide and friend.

Christ our Lord, you walk beside us, giving daily work to do;
Years go by and still you guide us as we seek to follow you.
If our sight fails, weak hands tremble, minds forget the things we've known,
Lord, we trust that you'll remember, hold us close, and see us home.

Tune: HYMN TO JOY 87.87 D ("Joyful, Joyful, We Adore Thee"), Ludwig van Beethoven, 1824.
Alternative Tune: IN BABILONE

You Formed Us in Your Image, Lord

This hymn was written for Carlisle (Pennsylvania) Presbytery's Discover & Connect event on family ministries where my husband and co-pastor Bruce and I gave the keynote presentation and were workshop leaders. The Advisory Committee on Social Witness Policy (ACSWP)'s 2004 report, "Transforming Families," was helpful as I was writing this hymn for ministry with families. The hymn was later included in the study action guide to that report, posted on the PC(USA) web site (*www.pcusa.org*). Biblical texts include: Genesis 1:26-27; Galatians 3:26-27, 5:1; Acts 16:30-34; Ephesians 4:15; Mark 3:32-35; Matthew 6:33; 2 Timothy 1:5; and Acts 2.

Our Christian understanding of "family" begins with the belief that each one of us is created in the image of God, and that God loves each one of us uniquely. Consider the meaning of family in your life and experience:

> What are the strengths that you see in families you know?
> How do homes you know honor God, with love as a strong foundation?
> How was your faith formed in the home you grew up in?
> In your church?
> What families do you see where love and trust is shattered?
> What did Jesus teach about loyalty to our families and to God's
>   kingdom?

60. You Formed Us in Your Image, Lord

You formed us in your image, Lord; You call us your own children.
In you, each one is loved, adored—Unique among the millions.
Bless, Lord, the families Who know the joy: Christ claims and frees!
Bless, too, the ones who weep, Forgetting that you love them.

You made our homes to honor you, With love the strong foundation.
In serving God and neighbor too, We find our life's vocation.
Bless families large and small, Who love and serve you when you call.
Bless, too, the ones who fear—Whose trust and love are shattered.

Christ loved and honored family, Yet showed us what is greater.
He taught a higher loyalty To God our good Creator.
Bless, Lord, the ones who long To build up homes where faith is strong.
Bless children, women, men Who risk to serve your kingdom.

In home and church our faith is formed; We learn your love and caring.
From here we're called to face the storm, Your love and justice bearing.
Each day your Spirit sends! We go to strangers, neighbors, friends.
Peace, justice, joy we bring To all your human family.

Tune: GREENSLEEVES 87.87 with refrain ("What Child Is This"), English ballad, 16th century.

When Hands Reach Out

This hymn was commissioned for a national conference on disabilities hosted by Second Presbyterian Church in Little Rock, Arkansas. *Presbyterians for Disability Concerns* has posted it on their web site (*www.pcusa.org/phewa/pdc.htm*). This hymn was included in the United Church of Canada's hymnal supplement. Biblical references include John 15:15 and 1 Corinthians 12.

I am grateful for the ministry of many people who have touched my life over the years. One of them is Jessie Scanlon, a young woman with autism. She was a teenager when we were serving the church she attended with her family. Every Sunday, she, her sister and parents would sit near the front of the sanctuary, on the left hand side. She had her own ministry there. She reminded us that God's "love is a gift, and never earned."

I am grateful for the ministry of one person who has sight problems and another who has hearing difficulties. They have taught me that hands can sing, and that love relies on gifts other than sight and sound.

I am grateful for the ministry of a friend who faced a terminal illness. He lived and died as a person with deep faith in God's abiding love. All of these friends, and many others, have helped me to understand God's care and unconditional love.

61. When Hands Reach Out

When hands reach out and fingers trace
The beauty of a loved one's face,
We thank you, God, that love relies
On gifts of grace not seen with eyes.

When fingers spell and signs express
Our prayer and praise and thankfulness,
We thank you, God, that hands can sing;
You bless the silent songs we bring.

When broken bodies will not mend,
We thank you, God, for Christ our Friend.
In him, our healing can begin:
He welcomes all the wounded in.

And when the ways we learn and grow
Are not the ways that others know,
We thank you, God, that we have learned
Your love's a gift, and never earned.

Your Spirit gives us differing ways
To serve you well and offer praise.
When all are joined as one, we'll be
Your able, strong community.

Tune: O WALY WALY LM ("Though I May Speak"), English folk melody.
Alternate Tune: TALLIS' CANON

O God, Our Creator, You Work Every Day

This hymn was written to be sung on Labor Day weekend. I found some helpful insights for writing it in the PC(USA) General Assembly 1995 Report "God's Work in Our Hands" and United Presbyterian Church in the USA General Assembly 1977 Report "That All May Enter." See Psalm 121:4; John 5:17; Isaiah 64:8; John 10:1-18; Luke 15:3-7; Luke 15:11-32; Mark 6:3; Luke 9:58; Matthew 11:28-30; Micah 6:8; Psalm 9:9; Isaiah 65:20-22; 1 John 3:1, 4:10; Romans 5:8; Galatians 3:27; Ephesians 2:7-10; 1 Corinthians 12:4-7; John 13:31-35; 15:12; 2 Corinthians 5:19.

As Christians, we celebrate God's work in creating the world and in creating us in God's image. We remember Jesus' very human work as a carpenter who got tired like everyone else.

We remember as well the work of ordinary people today. Many are simply trying to care for their families, working at jobs that are unfulfilling. Some are doing dangerous work for the benefit of us all. Some work hard, yet face oppressive working conditions and inadequate pay.

We also celebrate and thank God for the gifts of people who can't work in the traditional sense but who still have a vocation of teaching us to love. We remember those "whose work is to make us more humbly aware. They teach us the best of your lessons, by far: It's not what we do, Lord, you love who we are!"

God calls us, giving us gifts to use for the good of all, and work to do. Sometimes we work for pay and sometimes we voluntarily use our gifts to serve others. How has the work you have done in life been satisfying to you? How have you understood your work as a calling or vocation from God?

62. O God, Our Creator, You Work Every Day

O God, our Creator, you work every day:
A potter, you form us, your people, like clay.
A shepherd, you guide us and seek out the lost.
A parent, you love us, not counting the cost.

Christ Jesus, how rough were your hard-working hands!
You labored among us; our God understands!
Bless workers who struggle, their families to feed;
Bless those who face hardship, oppression, or greed.

Lord, some live among us who need constant care,
Whose work is to make us more humbly aware.
They teach us the best of your lessons, by far:
It's not what we do, Lord, you love who we are!

We're baptized! Your Spirit gives new work to do,
That we, through our serving, may glorify you.
Each person's vocation, each calling, has worth
As you send us out to bring Christ's love on earth.

Tune: ST. DENIO 11.11.11.11 ("Immortal, Invisible, God Only Wise"), Welsh Folk Hymn, adapted in *Caniadau y Cyssegr*, 1839
Alternate Tune: FOUNDATION
Text: Copyright © 2000 by Carolyn Winfrey Gillette. All rights reserved.

God, Bless the Poet's Heart and Hand

Many of the biblical references that go with this hymn speak about our need for humility before God. "I am who I am," says God. Our words cannot contain who God is. Our understanding of the Bible, our human knowledge and our obedience are never great enough that we can say we have all the answers. "For now, we see in a mirror dimly, but then we will see face to face . . . " (1 Corinthians 13:12). See also: Psalm 96; Exodus 3:14, Job 38-39, John 3:8, Psalm 119:105, 2 Timothy 3:16, Luke 4:20-30, 1 John 1:8, Ephesians 2:8-10, 1 Peter 5:5-6, 2 Corinthians 5:16-17, and John 16:13.

It is a joy for me to put faith into words that other people sing in worship. But it is also important for all of us to remember that words, even our best words, are not an end in themselves. One does not write so other people will say, "What great words you have written!" Words are tools for expressing faith and hope and love; yet we always need to be reminded that our human words are limited expressions of what we believe about God—and that God is far greater than anything our words can contain.

Our understanding of scripture is at best limited, and we need to be open to the insights of others. No one person or church has all the answers about God. Our own knowledge should never impress us so much that we think we have the only truth. Our community, church, and national leaders should never feel they have all the answers or the right to do as they please. Like the rest of us, they are simply ones who serve others. 1 Corinthians 13:12 reminds us, "For now we see in a mirror, dimly, but then we will see face to face." One day we will stand in the presence of God and simply say, "Your love and truth are greater than anything I could have imagined or thought or understood! Thank you, God, for loving me!"

63. God, Bless the Poet's Heart and Hand

God, bless the poet's heart and hand, creating songs of faith and praise;
Yet may each writer understand our words cannot contain your ways.

God, bless the ones who boldly dare to let the scriptures be their guide;
Yet may no one of us declare that you are always on our side.

God, bless the ones who teach and learn, who seek the truth by which to live;
Yet show us: Knowledge cannot earn the love that only you can give.

God, bless the ones who daily lead your churches, cities, nations, too;
Yet may these leaders humbly see their need to serve and follow you.

In Christ we daily live and grow; your Spirit guides us by your grace.
A mirrored image now we know; yet one day we'll see face to face.

Tune: TALLIS' CANON LM ("All Praise to Thee, My God, This Night"), Thomas Tallis, c. 1561

O God, Our Words Cannot Express

This hymn was written on September 11, 2001, as we were watching the TV news stories of the World Trade Center towers collapsing, the Pentagon being attacked, and the plane crashing in Western Pennsylvania. The hymn was shared widely on the Internet and was posted on the Web sites of the PC(USA) Church World Service, Evangelical Lutheran Church in America, United Methodist Committee On Relief, Church of Scotland's Presbytery of Glasgow, The Text This Week, Deacon Sil's Homiletic Resources Web site (Roman Catholic), CyberHymnal and many others. It appeared in *Presbyterians Today* magazine in November 2001. It was sung at memorial services for firefighters in New York City, and someone told me there was a stack of copies in Heathrow Airport. I was amazed by the places it appeared and the lives it touched.

A number of weeks after 9/11/2001, a large brown envelope arrived in our mailbox. It was from the church school children of a church in Canada; they had apparently gotten my address because of this hymn. Each child and teacher had written a letter expressing profound sorrow about what had happened on 9/11 and offering prayers for us in that time of tragedy. They asked me to share their letters with children in the United States. Emily, a sixth grader, wrote these words:

> "To the children of America—
> Within our tearful world, fear and evil be,
> The subject of our chatter, between both you and me.
> I pray for those you've lost and those who are in pain,
> I hope this never happens to anyone again.
> Don't worry about who you've lost,
> Whether they be he/she,
> For I know God is with them,
> So glory let there be. —Emily"

One of the Sunday school teachers wrote these words in her letter:

> "We will remain hopeful that out of this will be born a world more caring, a safer place for us all. —God bless you! Judy."

Words cannot express the pain we all felt that day. I treasure all of those church school children's and teachers' letters, and I am grateful that they found the words to share that day in their class. May we all work so that our compassion will shine through. May our leaders work with God's guidance to bring peace, and may our world be a more caring and safer place for us all. ❧

64. O God, Our Words Cannot Express

O God, our words cannot express
The pain we feel this day.
Enraged, uncertain, we confess
Our need to bow and pray.
We grieve for all who lost their lives . . .
And for each injured one.
We pray for children, husbands, wives
Whose grief has just begun.
O Lord, we're called to offer prayer
For all our leaders, too.
May they, amid such great despair,
Be wise in all they do.
We trust your mercy and your grace;
In you we will not fear!
May peace and justice now embrace!
Be with your people here!

Tune: St. Anne CM ("Our God, Our Help in Ages Past"), attr. William Croft, 1708.
Text: Copyright © 2001 by Carolyn Winfrey Gillette. All rights reserved.

God, We've Known Such Grief and Anger

This hymn commemorates the anniversary of September 11th. It was commissioned by Presbyterian Disaster Assistance and is included in their book *Out of the Depths: Voices of the Presbyterian Faith Community at Work after September 11*. I wrote it so that it could be used at times of other disasters, and sadly, people have found reasons to use it all too often, including after the shootings at Virginia Tech. Biblical references include Psalm 13:1-2, John 14:18, 1 John 4:7,8, 18.

One of the most powerful images in the Bible is that God calls us children. God adopts us and shows his eternal love for us through Jesus Christ. Jesus reminds us in the 14th chapter of John's gospel, "I will never leave you orphaned." Even in the most desolate, despairing times, we are not abandoned. God in Jesus Christ still loves us and holds us close.

And so we pray. We pray for fear to be replaced with love. We pray for wisdom and guidance and "sure direction." We pray for people who are grieving. We pray for rescue workers and volunteers. And we pray for glimpses of God's kingdom through it all.

65. God, We've Known Such Grief and Anger

God, we've known such grief and anger
As we've heard your people cry.
We have asked you, "How much longer?"
We have sadly wondered, "Why?"
In this world of so much suffering,
May we hear your word anew:
"I will never leave you orphaned;
I will not abandon you."

By your grace comes resurrection;
By your love, you cast out fear.
You give strength and sure direction
As we seek to serve you here.
You give comfort to the grieving,
And you bless the ones who mourn.
May we trust in you, believing
Out of chaos, hope is born.

Hope is ours for, God, you love us!
You have claimed us by your grace.
And through Jesus, you have called us
To bring hope to every place.
In each rescue worker's caring,
In each faithful volunteer,
In each Christian's love and sharing,
God, we glimpse your kingdom here.

Tune: IN BABILONE 87.87 D ("There's a Wideness in God's Mercy"), Dutch melody, arr. by Julius Rontgen, 1906

God of Creation

On August 29, 2005, Hurricane Katrina devastated much of the Gulf Coast of the United States. Many people experienced terrible loss as individuals and as communities. Many others of us watched on television and wondered at what had happened and why. This hymn is one that I wrote early on in this tragedy when the poor government response and concerns related to racism in the response had not fully come to light. Biblical references include Genesis 1, Psalm 13, Matthew 8:23-27, 25:31-46; Luke 10:25-37

As Christians, we look at life not just through TV screens or even through first-hand experiences, but through the lenses of our faith. We ask questions of God who created everything. We may confess our doubts and our sense of being forsaken. We turn to Christ and ask for his powerful, loving presence. We hear in the events of this world the call and empowerment of the Holy Spirit to serve our neighbors.

Our church is one of many that sent a team of volunteers to the Gulf Coast to help in the rebuilding efforts after Hurricane Katrina. It was a joy for church members and friends to be able to work with one particular woman in renovating her house for her, her children and grandchildren. The rebuilding efforts will be going on for many years; God continues to call churches to serve by building houses and building relationships.

What has been your response to tragedy in your life or community? How has God given you faith to get through challenging times, and strength to respond in love to others who are hurting?

66. God of Creation

God of creation, We have seen the horror—
Great devastation, Overwhelming sorrow!
Hear now your people—Homes and loved ones taken—
Feeling forsaken.

Christ of compassion, You who calmed the rough sea—
Hurricane crashing, We prayed for your mercy!
Comfort your people! Hold them close, now giving
Hope for their living.

Give to your children Food to end their hunger,
Clean water's blessing, News of those they long for!
And by your Spirit, Use our gifts and labors
To help our neighbors.

Tune: HERZLIEBSTER JESU 11 11 11.5 ("Ah, Holy Jesus"). Johann Cruger, 1640
Text: Copyright © 2005 by Carolyn Winfrey Gillette. All rights reserved.

God, You Give Us Recreation

This hymn was written for Souper Bowl Sunday worship and celebrations each year. It has gotten wide use because of its posting on the websites of Souper Bowl Sunday, Church World Service, and many denominational hunger programs. See Exodus 20:8, 34:21, 16:22-30; Ecclesiastes 3:12-13, 9:7-9; Deuteronomy 15:11; Amos 5:24; Mark 6:34-44; Matthew 6:10.

The Souper Bowl of Caring website tells how Brad Smith, a seminary intern serving at Spring Valley Presbyterian Church in Columbia, South Carolina, offered a simple prayer on Super Bowl Sunday: "Lord, even as we enjoy the Super Bowl football game, help us be mindful of those who are without a bowl of soup to eat." That prayer was the beginning of a movement led primarily by youth to help hungry people around the world. In many churches and communities across the United States, Super Bowl Sundays became Souper Bowl Sundays, a time of football, fun, and collecting money in soup pots to be used for food pantries in local communities and hunger causes around the world. Cans of food are also collected.

Many of us love the fun celebrations in our lives—the Super Bowl parties, the Fourth of July picnics, the birthday parties for young and old, the anniversary celebrations. What are some ways you acknowledge God's presence in these special times in your life, family and community?

67. God, You Give Us Recreation

God, you give us recreation, rest and play when work is through,
Game and sport and celebration, times that challenge and renew.
In the days we spend together, in the feasts that we prepare,
In the times of joy and laughter, may we know your loving care.

Yet, O Lord, we see you crying for the ones who know no rest,
For your children, hungry, dying, for the homeless and oppressed.
May we, as your sons and daughters, share with open heart and hand,
Till your justice flows like water to the poor throughout the land.

Bless, O Christ, our gifts of caring, for we know without a doubt:
Soup and bread are made for sharing, hands are made for reaching out.
Even in our times of playing, may we keep the vision clear:
Keep us serving, loving, praying, welcoming your kingdom here.

Tune: IN BABILONE 87.87 D ("There's a Wideness in God's Mercy"), Dutch Melody arr. by Julius Rontgen, 1906

Giving God, We Pause and Wonder

This hymn is appropriate for use whenever a church considers the meaning of Christian stewardship. Biblical references include: Malachi 3:8-10, Romans 15:25-26, and 1 John 4:7-8.

Often when we talk about giving to the church, we wonder what we "should" give. What is "enough" to help us grow in our faith and reach out to others? A better question might be, "What could the church do, if we dreamed big? What would happen if we took seriously the biblical call to give ten percent of our income?"

At the Massanetta Springs Bible Conference a couple of years ago, I heard a powerful sermon by a Presbyterian minister named the Rev. Tony Tian-Ren Lin, who is also a doctoral student in sociology at the University of Virginia. He talked about what could happen if every Christian (or even most of us) routinely gave ten percent of our income to the church for its ministries of love and compassion. He quoted Ron Sider's book, *The Scandal of the Evangelical Conscience.* Tony said, "According to Sider, the average household income in the U.S. is $42,000-plus. If every American who claims to be a Christian tithed, we'd have about $143 billion a year. UNICEF said it would cost $70-80 billion a year to provide food, healthcare and education for all the poor children of the world. Can you imagine if American Christians went to the UN and said 'We'll pick up the tab.' We could pay for food, healthcare and education for all the children in the world and *still* have $70 billion left to run our ministries here and send missionaries there. Imagine the implications of this if we as a denomination decided to do this. Imagine that every Presbyterian began tithing and PC(USA) began sending billions of dollars around the world to help the poor and the sick. Imagine that day when people around the world see the PC(USA) seal and immediately associate it with those who love their neighbors as themselves."

Both these authors know that our giving should never be a way of saying, "Look what we've done!" or "Look what we can do!" Our gifts are simply a way of saying "thank you" to God. Yet, what a wonderful witness a tithing church would be of God's love in a hurting world. How can you say thank you to God today, as you share God's gifts to you with someone else? ❦

68. Giving God, We Pause and Wonder

Giving God, we pause and wonder: What would happen if we tithed—
If we gave our gifts, Creator, hearts and hands all opened wide?
We might learn, by gladly sharing, Not to trust in things we own
But to risk—it's part of caring—And to trust in you alone.

We could do abundant mission, Sharing Christ who claims and frees.
We could reach out with new vision In creative ministries.
No more bound by limitations Of what churches can't afford,
We could learn with jubilation Whole new ways to serve you, Lord.

In each country that was struggling, We could build a thousand schools,
We could feed a million orphans And give countless farmers tools.
As we gladly shared your blessings, Then the world might want to know:
"See! How loving are those Christians! Who's the One who makes them so?"

God, we know we cannot pay you For your love in Christ your Son.
Gifts and tithes are just a "thank you"—Ways to pass your blessings on.
We have learned that, in our sharing, We receive more than we give.
By your Spirit, make us daring, In this joyful way to live.

Tune: NETTLETON 87.87 D ("Come Thou Fount of Every Blessing"), Wyeth's *Repository of Sacred Music*, 1813

"If Only I Had Known"

This was commissioned by Bob Kruschwitz, director of the Center on Christian Ethics at Baylor University, as part of the Global Wealth issue of the Center's quarterly journal, *Christian Reflection*. The challenges of globalization and the disparity between the rich and the poor continue to be issues with which western Christians need to struggle. See Luke 16:19-31; Luke12:13-21; and Deuteronomy 15:11-12. This hymn is appropriate for a Mission Sunday.

The "wide gap" that exists is not just the one between the rich man and Lazarus after they both die. On five mission trips to Honduras, one of the poorest countries in the Western Hemisphere, I have been reminded of the wide gap between rich and poor that exists right now. Many of us cannot begin to understand. I remember hearing a sermon by a lay preacher in one village. Preaching on the passage, "I was hungry and you fed me . . .", he said, "If your neighbor's children are hungry, and all you have left is two days' worth of flour for tortillas, it is your responsibility as a Christian to share some of your flour with your neighbor." How can those of us with bank accounts and retirement funds begin to comprehend this?

On one of those trips to Honduras, a church worker in the capital city of Tegucigalpa was speaking to our church group. He said, "God has brought you here for a reason—not to be a tourist, not to have a vacation—but for a reason. Your job, here in Honduras, is to find out what that reason is."

When have you experienced the troubling imbalance between rich and poor in this world? How have you seen the connections between what you eat, drink, wear, and use, and how other people in the world live? The rich man in the hymn says, "If only I had known." We do know a lot about the global economy and how it affects people whose lives touch ours. Since we know, what is God calling us to do about it? ❦

69. "If Only I Had Known"

"If only I had known the cost of human greed,
Perhaps I would have reached out more to those in need.
But now I see the truth across the great divide!
If only I had known and changed," the rich man cried.

If only we could see which bargains in the store
Are made in dismal sweatshops that oppress the poor.
For each subsistence wage—each tiny, crippling stitch—
Makes wider the divide between the poor and rich.

And, too, if we could hear a mother's lullaby;
She's singing now to calm her hungry toddler's cry.
For rich ones came one day, took land and water rights,
And left the poor with hopeless days and hungry nights.

If only we could learn what keeps us wanting more:
We build our bigger barns so we'll feel more secure.
But you alone, O God, give true security;
Possessed by our possessions, we cannot be free.

O Christ, if we could know God's will for all the earth!
And yet, by your own Spirit, you have shown God's truth:
"Do justice, help the poor, share life and love and land,
And when you see the hungry, open wide your hand."

Tune: LEONI 66.84D ("The God of Abraham Praise"), Hebrew melody, adapt. by Thomas Olivers and Meyer Lyon, 1770.

Text: Carolyn Winfrey Gillette, 2007

God, How Can We Comprehend?

According to Church World Service's website, "nearly 33 million people around the world are uprooted from their homes and communities by persecution and armed conflict." (*www.churchworldservice.org*) The lines of refugees in this world are seemingly endless. This hymn was written as a prayer for those refugees and for those of us in the church who are called to reach out in God's love. Biblical references: Luke 15:1, Matthew 25:31-46, John 3:16; Colossians 1:20; John 14:26-27

When we see tragedies on the news, we often see things that are happening on a massive scale. We see the war in the Sudan, the tsunami in Asia, and the chaos wherever people flee their countries due to war and violence. We see pictures of long lines of people carrying their possessions, people crowding around supply trucks, and tent cities in the middle of the desert. Each one of those people in each one of those crowds is a child of God, loved by God. Long lines of refugees are made up on people who have music in their souls and dreams for their children.

Many churches in the United States look for ways to respond to massive tragedy by helping people on a very personal level. Some may sponsor refugee families in their communities. Others may teach English to people who are new to the United States and who need these language skills. Some try to help people struggling across desert borders in the Southwest. Still others go on mission trips, and form ongoing relationships with communities in other parts of the world. These personal connections can be filled with joy, learning and friendship. Of course it is good when our churches can help people in need on a massive scale, yet it is also helpful to be reminded that all God's children have names, faces and songs to sing.

70. God, How Can We Comprehend?

God, how can we comprehend—
Though we've seen them times before—
Lines of people without end
Fleeing danger, want, and war?
They seek safety anywhere,
Hoping for a welcome hand!
Can we know the pain they bear?
Help us, Lord, to understand!

You put music in their souls;
Now they struggle to survive.
You gave each one gifts and goals;
Now they flee to stay alive.
God of outcasts, may we see
How you value everyone,
For each homeless refugee
Is your daughter or your son.

Lord, your loving knows no bounds;
You have conquered death for all.
May we hear beyond our towns
To our distant neighbors' call.
Spirit, may our love increase;
May we reach to all your earth,
Till your whole world lives in peace;
Till we see each person's worth.

Tune: ABERYSTWYTH 77.77 D ("Watchman, Tell Us of the Night"), Joseph Parry, 1879.
Text: Copyright © by Carolyn Winfrey Gillette, 1999, rev. ed. 2001. All rights reserved.

God, May Your Justice Roll Down

This hymn was commissioned by the Presbyterian Historical Society to go with the theme of Presbyterian Heritage Sunday in 2001. It was mailed out to all the PC(USA) churches for their use on that occasion, and has been used by many churches since that time. See Amos 5:24.

"God, May Your Justice Roll Down" is based on Amos 5:24: "Let justice roll down like waters and righteousness like an ever-flowing stream." Through the centuries, countless numbers of God's people have worked for just that. They have worked for reforms in education, sought to end oppression, worked in ministries of healing, and struggled to bring civil rights to all people. Who are the saints of old who have inspired you? Are they famous people you read about in books and learned about in school? Are they your grandparents and great-grandparents who worked in communities you know and care about? How has justice rolled down like waters—waters that can't be stopped—because of the work and witness of the saints that you know? ᵂᵞ

71. God, May Your Justice Roll Down

God, may your justice roll down like the waters you send here,
And may your righteousness flow like a stream without end here!
Praying this prayer, many have struggled and dared,
All for the world you intend here.

Christ, we give thanks for past saints who renewed education,
Freed the oppressed, brought your healing and fought segregation.
Savior and Lord, great were the risks they endured,
Bearing your hope and salvation.

We as your church now remember these stories of others
And pray your Spirit will send us, as your sons and daughters.
Show us the way we, too, can serve you each day
Till justice rolls down like waters.

Tune: LOBE DEN HERREN 14.14.478 ("Praise Ye the Lord, the Almighty"), *Stralsund Erneuerten Gesangbuch*, 1665.

A Voice Was Heard in Ramah

This hymn was inspired by the sad news from the Middle East about the ongoing conflict between the Palestinians and the Israelis, and by the news stories that come out of our own cities and towns. It was included in the United Church of Canada's hymnal supplement. It is based on the end of the Christmas story in Matthew's gospel, a part of the story traditionally known as the "slaughter of the innocents." Biblical references include: Matthew 2:13-23; Romans 12:15; Matthew 25:31-46; Isaiah 9:6, Psalm 85:10.

Fear and anger bring so much suffering to the children of the world, as well as to others in their communities. In Matthew's Christmas story, Herod became angry when the wise men gave him news of a new king who had been born. He was afraid this new king might be competition for him. So he ordered all the children two years old and under to be killed. Matthew quotes from the prophet Jeremiah: "A voice was heard in Ramah, wailing and loud lamentation, Rachel weeping for her children; she refused to be consoled, because they are no more." (Matthew 2:18). In our world today, there are millions of parents weeping for their children, and thousands of communities where children are suffering every day because of violence. What is it like for a child to grow up surrounded by fighting and war? What is it like for little ones to go to bed with the sounds of weapons firing?

Some of us live in places where war seems far away. But we—and our children—are not free of violence either. It is in our cities, our schools, our families, and our life as a nation. Some of our recent leaders have emphasized fear and used it as a justification for national policies promoting violence. As Christians, we are called to work for God's peace and justice, for reconciliation, and for forgiveness. The Bible lifts up a vision of a time when peace and justice will embrace.

In God's good creation, when any of God's little ones suffer anywhere in the world, life is diminished for the rest of us, too. Yet we have hope—hope that comes from God—that one day peace and justice will embrace. ❦

72. A Voice Was Heard in Ramah

A voice was heard in Ramah that could not be consoled,
As Rachel wept for children she could no longer hold.
For Herod ruled the nation, yet feared the Infant King.
How great the devastation that fear and anger bring!

O God, we hear the crying for little ones of yours;
For many still are dying in conflicts and in wars—
In every troubled nation, on every violent street,
How great the lamentation when fear and anger meet!

Whenever one is weeping, the whole world suffers, too.
Yet, Jesus, as we serve them, we're also serving you.
So may we not ignore them, nor turn our eyes away,
But help us labor for them to bring a better day.

O Prince of Peace, you lead us in ways of truth and grace.
May we be brave to practice your peace in every place—
To love each fear-filled nation, to serve each troubled street.
How great the celebration when peace and justice meet!

Tune: LLANGLOFFAN 7 6.7 6 D ("O God of Earth and Altar"), Welsh Folk Melody. Alternate Tune:
PASSION CHORALE

Another Son Is Killed

This hymn is dedicated to the memory of Shaul Lahav, grandson of Paul and Helen Loeb, who was killed on November 18, 2003 on the road between Bethlehem and Jerusalem. See Psalm 137:1-2 and Isaiah 2:4.

Early one Tuesday morning, we got the phone call from grandparents in our church that their grandson had been killed in Israel. Shaul had been staffing a checkpoint on the road between Bethlehem and Jerusalem with another Israeli soldier. A Palestinian had come toward them with a prayer rug. Hidden within it was an automatic weapon. He killed Shaul and the other soldier while the latter was talking on a cell phone to his mother. My husband and co-pastor Bruce went over to the Loeb's house and prayed with them that morning. Later in the day, he took them to the airport so they could attend their grandson's funeral in Israel. The following Sunday, this hymn was sung in our church, and shared with Shaul's family in Israel.

Because of Bruce's work in the Presbyterian Church's General Assembly related to the Middle East, we are very much aware that there are tragic killings and suffering experienced by all sides, including many of our fellow Christians who are Palestinians. Loved ones on all sides of conflicts get those terrible phone calls. As people of faith, we pray for peace, for a time when weapons of war will be transformed into farming tools and gardening implements, when national budgets will be used not to kill but to feed and care for people.

At least once a week in worship, and for many of us every day, we pray, "Thy kingdom come, thy will be done on earth as it is in heaven." What have you done today, to work for God's kingdom of peace and justice? What can you and your church do? ❧

73. Another Son Is Killed

Another son is killed,
Another daughter dies,
And loving, waiting homes are filled
With loved ones' cries.
As rivers never sleep,
So wars flow on and on.
Hang up your harps, sit down and weep
For those now gone!

We grieve for children lost,
For hearts too sad to pray;
We mourn, O Lord, the growing cost
Of hatred's way.
And sure as threats increase
And anger turns to war,
We pray that we may find a peace
Worth struggling for.

We know your way, O Lord,
For all your people here:
A plowshare from a fighting sword,
A transformed spear!
Now comfort those who grieve,
Be in each saddened home,
And by your grace may we believe—
And seek Shalom.

Tune: LEONI 66.84 ("The God of Abraham Praise"), Hebrew melody adapt. by Thomas Olivers and Meyer Lyon, 1770.

Text: Copyright © 2003 by Carolyn Winfrey Gillette. All rights reserved.

Blest Are God's Peacemaking Ones

Jesus said, "Blessed are those who hunger and thirst for righteousness, for they will be filled . . . Blessed are the peacemakers, for they will be called children of God" (Matthew 5:6,9). See also Matthew 13:33 and Luke 13:20-21.

A few years ago, I heard a news story from the Pittsburgh area about a kind, gentle man of faith who was killed in a violent, senseless attack in an apartment building. He had worked for years on behalf of people in that city who are poor. Since then, there have been other news stories of peacemakers in other communities who have put their lives on the line to share the good news of God's love with people who are hurting.

Jesus said that peacemakers are blessed, for they will be called the children of God. He talked of people hungering and thirsting for righteousness. There are some among us who have the courage to stand, say, and do what is right, even when it is unpopular or dangerous to do so. Jesus used the wonderful image of leaven in the bread. It just takes a little leaven to lighten the whole loaf. In the same way, a few determined, dedicated Christians sharing God's love can make a world of difference—in Pittsburgh, or in any community in the world. 🌾

74. Blest Are God's Peacemaking Ones

Blest are God's peacemaking ones, Sent to work in countless ways—
God's own daughters, God's own sons, Serving without seeking praise.
Yet like leaven in our bread, They persist to change us all.
By God's Spirit, they are led To pursue God's peaceful call.

Bless-ed are God's prophets, too, Called to challenge what we know.
Working for a world that's new, Calling us to change and grow.
Though the message that they bear Stands against what powers say—
It is Jesus' word they share, News of God's new breaking day.

God, through Jesus' love and grace, May we live what we profess.
In the challenges we face, May we know what makes us blest.
May we stand against the wrong; May our thirst for you increase.
Give to us a prophet's song! May we work to bring your peace!

Tune: ABERYSTWYTH 77.77 D ("Watchman, Tell Us of the Night"), Joseph Parry, 1879

"Lord, What is All Our Fighting For?"

One of the news stories that came out of the Iraq war many months ago was of a young girl who witnessed her parents being shot dead at a checkpoint. This hymn was written to remember that child and her parents and all people who suffer in wars. In the face of the tragedy of war, Christians must speak out for a biblical vision of what God desires for this world. See Micah 4:3; 6:8; Isaiah 2:4 and Matthew 5:9.

How has war changed our perception of what is acceptable in this world, and what is not? Have we become numb to the stories we see in the news, of both civilians and soldiers being killed and wounded? Most of us hear the news and, unless we are directly affected, shake our heads and go back to the daily business of our lives. Instead, should we be marching, writing letters to people in Congress, holding prayer vigils for all the people involved? World conflicts are surely complicated and people have different opinions about what the right thing to do really is, but shouldn't Christians be doing something more? Shouldn't we be paying more attention?

What if people around the world could routinely say, "I know you Christians. I know what you stand for. Jesus taught you to be peacemakers. Thank you for trying to change the world for the better."

Micah 6:8 reminds us, "What does the Lord require of you but to do justice, and to love kindness, and to walk humbly with your God?" When we do these things, we will cry out for the world to be more what God wants it to be.

How have you been bold to say, "No more!" to things that go against God's way?

75. Lord, What Is All Our Fighting For?

Lord, what is all our fighting for?
We train our young to go to war.
A young girl sees the terror spread
As soldiers shoot her parents dead.

Lord, what is our acceptance for?
We tolerate what you abhor.
Each day more little ones are lost;
May we seek truth and count war's cost.

What can we for repentance bring?
You do not want an offering.
"Do what is just," you simply say;
"Love what is kind and seek my way."

Lord, what is all our silence for?
Now make us bold to say, "No more!"
The world need not be what it's been;
Your peace will reign! Your love will win!

Tune: O Waly Waly LM ("Though I May Speak"), English folk melody
Alternate Tune: Tallis' Canon

O God, Each Day You Bless Us

Mark Koenig of the Presbyterian Peacemaking Program wanted a hymn that would celebrate the anniversary of the Commitment to Peacemaking. "O God, Each Day You Bless Us" lifts up the themes found in this commitment about what local congregations can be doing to further God's peace in the world. The hymn is a response to the words of Jesus, "Blessed are the peacemakers, for they will be called children of God" (Matthew 5:9).

What is your church doing in the area of peacemaking? Do your worship, prayer and study reflect your commitment? Do you reach out to others around the world? Do you care for the earth? Do you give generously?

What are you doing as an individual? Try writing your own commitment to peacemaking. Why do things like peace and justice matter? What will you do to worship, pray, study, reach out, care and give for peace and justice? How does what you do make a real difference for others?

76. O God, Each Day You Bless Us

O God, each day you bless us with gifts of your shalom:
You give us peace and justice, you welcome lost ones home.
You care for your creation and set your people free;
You offer us salvation and build community.

You make us sons and daughters—baptized and reconciled!
You show us each peacemaker is blest as your own child.
You fill us at your table with strength for each new day;
Then Spirit-filled we're able to live your peaceful way.

We'll worship, pray and study, to learn new skills for peace;
We'll work as one strong body so justice will increase.
We'll build new global friendships, seek peace in every land,
Protect the earth you gave us and give with outstretched hand.

You give your church a vision, a way of life, a prayer:
Your will is done in heaven; now bring in your reign here!
And when we wonder, grieving, at what the nations do,
God, may we work, believing there's hope in serving you.

Tune: LANCASHIRE 7.6.7.6 D ("The Day of Resurrection"), Henry Thomas Smart, 1835.
Alternate Tune: LLANGLOFFAN

God Whose Love Is Always Stronger

This hymn was written during the brief time after President George W. Bush issued the ultimatum to Saddam Hussein and before the war in Iraq actually began. Despite the efforts of many Christians, the United States went to war, violating the historic just war teaching that most major Christian churches have followed, and certainly violating the teachings of pacifist churches. This hymn, a prayer for peace, has grown in popularity as more and more Christians have reconsidered their earlier support for this war. Sojourners community included the hymn in its online resources, as did the National Council of Churches and Church World Service. The United Methodist Church posted it online with the music.

"God Whose Love Is Always Stronger" has many biblical references, including: Romans 8:28-39, 2 Corinthians 12:9, John 3:7, Revelation 21:5, 1 Corinthians 13:4-5, John 14:27, Matthew 5-7, 1 Thessalonians 2:2, John 3:16, 17:18, Psalm 46:9, and Romans 8:22.

"Love is patient; love is kind; love is not envious or boastful or arrogant or rude. It does not insist on its own way; it is not irritable or resentful; it does not rejoice in wrong-doing, but rejoices in the truth" (1 Corinthians 13:4-6). If we believe these words are God's truth, then we will also realize they are not just words that relate to our individual lives. They will also influence how we work for public policy.

What does it mean for Christians and for churches to say that love is patient . . . love is kind . . . love is not arrogant . . . love rejoices in the truth? We do not claim to have all the answers, but we have a vision for peace and a hope given to us by God who loves this whole world. William Sloane Coffin, Jr. once said, "The church's job is to proclaim, 'Let justice roll down like waters, and righteousness like an ever-flowing stream;' the government's job is to develop the irrigation system."

In what areas do we need to find courage and the time in our busy lives to speak truth to our leaders about important issues that mean life and death to thousands and thousands of people?

The first hymn in this book began with a proclamation: "The earth is the Lord's and the fullness thereof." The last hymn in the book ends with the prayer: "Give us love that we may share it till your love renews the earth." God is with us from the beginning of creation to the time when God's kingdom will come in all its fullness. In the meantime, God's grace fills our lives, and we are sent out to love our neighbors, to seek God's kingdom, and to witness to Jesus Christ who is the light of the world. Thanks be to God!

77. God Whose Love Is Always Stronger

God whose love is always stronger Than our weakness, pride and fear,
In your world, we pray and wonder How to be more faithful here.
Hate too often grows inside us; Fear rules what the nations do.
So we pray, when wars divide us: Give us love, Lord! Make us new!
Love is patient, kind and caring, Never arrogant or rude,
Never boastful, all things bearing; Love rejoices in the truth.
When we're caught up in believing War will make the terror cease,
Show us Jesus' way of living; May our strength be in your peace.
May our faith in you be nourished; May your churches hear your call.
May our lives be filled with courage As we speak your love for all.
Now emboldened by your Spirit Who has given us new birth,
Give us love, that we may share it Till your love renews the earth.

Tune: BEACH SPRING 87.87 D ("God, Whose Giving Knows No Ending"), The *Sacred Harp*, 1844.
Alternate Tunes: ABBOT'S LEIGH, HYFRYDOL

Appendix: Why We Sing[1]

Why do we sing in worship, rather than merely think or talk with one another? Singing is essential to the formation of Christian communities and the moral formation of each disciple, for "congregational song is by nature corporate, corporeal, and inclusive," suggests Brian Wren. "At its best, it is creedal, ecclesial, inspirational, and evangelical."[2]

As parts of the southern United States struggle to recover from the devastation caused by hurricanes Katrina and Rita, there are many images that stay in our minds, either from seeing these catastrophes first-hand, from listening to people who experienced them, or from watching the evening news. One particularly striking image on the news after Katrina was of a hospital staff struggling to care for patients when the medical facility no longer had electricity, water, food, or medicine to offer. There was one especially poignant picture from inside that hospital. In the midst of that horrible situation, several medical staff members were gathered around a patient's bed. They were singing songs of faith and of trust in the only One who could be counted on to help them. They were singing hymns that some of them had most likely learned by being in church Sunday after Sunday throughout their lives, where they had sung hymns until the words and music had become part of their very being. There in the midst of the storm-damaged hospital, in the midst of what has been described as "hell on earth," they were singing together, heavenward.

Why do we sing in worship rather than merely think or talk with one another? We sing because music is a gift from God. It is a language and a means that God has given us to express our deepest longings, our greatest joys, and our most profound trust in the One who created us and loves us unconditionally. Like all gifts from God, it is one that God calls us to use with gratitude.

A new hymn, "All the Music Sung and Played Here," written to the tune of NETTLE-TON ("Come, Thou Fount of Every Blessing"), can express our thanks to God for the gifts of music and singing in worship. The hymn begins with these words:

> All the music sung and played here is a gift, O God, from you.
> For as long as we have prayed here, we've been blessed by music, too.

By your Spirit, each musician finds new depths of faith to share.
Music is a gift you've given and becomes our thankful prayer.
("All The Music Sung and Played Here," first stanza)[3]

In *A Song To Sing, A Life to Live: Reflections on Music as Spiritual Practice,* Don Saliers points out that the gift of music is built into the very being of our bodies and of our lives—our heartbeats, breath, cries and movements. Young children love to bang pots and pans together. Children play chanting games as they jump rope together.[4] God has given us gifts of sound and music within us and around us. It is a short step to carry these gifts into our worship of God. Brian Wren says that congregational song is, among other things, "corporeal." "When we sing from the heart, with full voice, some of us use our bodies more thoroughly, perhaps, than at any other time in worship."[5]

We sing because music brings us together as a church. It brings together generations. Even young children who are part of the worshiping community can find a welcome in the church's singing together. Familiar songs and refrains invite preliterate children to participate. Songs of the church bring together people from diverse cultural backgrounds. Those who share the pews may have vastly different lives, but when they stand and sing, they share the faith that binds them together—God's love expressed in Jesus Christ, through the power of the Holy Spirit.

We sing because our singing is a means by which God strengthens us and helps us to grow as the people of God. In our individual lives, we may say and sing "I." But the songs of the church invite us to say "we." They call us to celebrate the faith that we share, and we are reminded of our place in the community of disciples.

We sing because, as those medical staff members in a New Orleans hospital knew, singing is one of many ways that God has given us to cry out in utter despair and in complete trust. Saint Augustine once said that the one who sings "prays twice."[6] Sometimes our psalms, hymns, and spiritual songs become our "thankful prayers" and other times they become our desperate prayers, prayers of lament, or prayers of trust and commitment.

We sing because singing connects Sunday worship with everyday life. Thomas G. Long points out: "In the place of worship, we cannot pray or sing faithfully without our words being full of the sorrows and joys of life. Conversely, the words of worship, prayer words, sermon words, hymn words, Bible words, creedal words, words of praise and penitence, protest and pardon—are like stones thrown into the pond; they ripple outward in countless concentric circles, finding ever fresh expression in new places in our lives."[7] We sing "Amazing Grace" together on a Sunday morning, and it changes us and makes us a little more grace-filled throughout the week in ways that are beyond our understanding.

We sing because God calls us to sing! The Psalmist proclaims: "O come, let us sing to the Lord; let us make a joyful noise to the rock of our salvation!" (Psalm 95:1). "Make a joyful noise to the Lord, all the earth. Worship the Lord with gladness; come into his presence with singing" (Psalm 100:1). In Colossians, we are instructed, "with gratitude in your hearts sing psalms, hymns, and spiritual songs to God" (Colossians 3:16).

> All creation sings your glory; in the Psalms are pain and praise.
> Mary sang your saving story in her long, expectant days.
> Through the years, with great emotion, some have reached to you in song.
> May we sing with such devotion; music helps your church grow strong!
> ("All the Music Sung and Played Here," second stanza)

One of the ways that our singing strengthens the church is by helping us to see our place in the body of Christ, where members are given different gifts to use for the good of all. If all the church were sopranos, where would the tenors be? If all the church were a chancel choir, where would the children's choir be? When Christians sing together, the blending of our voices bears witness to the fact that we are made one in Christ. The variety of voices (high, low, on key, off key, some soaring to the rafters, and some barely singing above a whisper) reminds us of the wonderful diversity in the church. Ed Norman writes "For Christians of all levels of musical attainment, there is the unique opportunity to sing in communal worship, where the critical ingredient is the attitude of the heart. There is an interesting metaphor for the church in group music making: working together under leadership to achieve a common goal of harmony and unity"[8] We are reminded, too, that there is a place in the body of Christ for those who cannot sing or speak, for those who are uncomfortable singing, for those who sing off key, for those who prefer to listen, for those who offer praise through sign language. God provides a wonderful variety of ways of offer praise.

Songs are a way by which we can express what we believe about God; at the same time, through songs, our faith is formed. Plato said, "Let me make the songs of a nation and I care not who makes the laws."[9] This statement has been quoted in modified form in relation to church music: "I don't mind who writes the theological books so long as I can write the hymns."[10] When we struggle to understand Christian beliefs, we often turn for help to songs that we have learned in church. Many church members would be at a loss to define "grace" without saying, "That reminds me of one of my favorite hymns, Amazing Grace . . . "

The songs we sing do not have to be complex to be wonderful expressions of what Christ's followers believe. "Jesus Loves Me" is one of the simplest songs, and one of the earliest ones that many Christian children learn to sing in church school. Yet if we take this simple children's song seriously, its message is profound. Karl Barth was once asked to summarize all his wealth of knowledge about the faith in one sentence, and he is said to have answered, "Jesus loves me, this I know, for the Bible tells me so."[11]

Some songs are specifically creedal; for example, there are several hymn texts of the Apostles' Creed (for one example, see "I Believe" in *Gifts of Love: New Hymns for Today's*

Worship).[12] Other songs help Christians express what the church believes in more informal ways, in the face of the world's conflicting values. Every day, Christians go out into workplaces and communities only to be bombarded with the idea that what we own and what we accomplish are the things that make us worthwhile as people. Then we go to church and sing, "Just as I am, without one plea . . . " The world too often teaches that wealth and power are the things that matter about us. Then we go to church and sing songs of faith like, "Lord, You Have Come to the Lakeshore":

> "You have come up to the lakeshore,
> Looking neither for wise nor for wealthy.
> You only wanted that I should follow.
> O Lord, with Your eyes You have search me,
> And, while smiling, have called out my name.
> Now my boat's left on the shoreline behind me,
> Now with You I will seek other seas."[13]

While these words are far from those of a traditional creed, they express ideas that are very central to what the church believes. God's love is not something we earn; it is freely and graciously given. Further, Jesus calls us to be faithful disciples.

Some hymns express the faith so clearly that they are threatening to those in power. Mary's song of praise, the Magnificat, contains these powerful words:

> "He has shown strength with his arm;
> He has scattered the proud in the thoughts of their hearts.
> He has brought down the powerful from their thrones, and lifted up the
>   lowly;
> He has filled the hungry with good things, and sent the rich away empty"
> (Luke 1:51-53).

Elizabeth A. Johnson points out that the Magnificat's message is so subversive that for a period during the 1980s the government of Guatemala banned its public recitation."[14] What powerful, rich leaders of nations would want large numbers of poor people to take those words seriously as a statement of belief? Patrick D. Miller, Jr. writes, "In a world that assumes the status is quo, that things have to be the way they are and that we must not assume too much about improving them, the doxologies of God's people are fundamental indicators that wonders have not ceased, that possibilities not yet dreamt of will happen, and that hope is an authentic stance."[15] When we sing as a church, we are affirming our faith that God is still active among us.

The songs we sing as a congregation teach us what it means to be the church, and they connect us to the church in a way that spoken words cannot easily do. Hymns and songs sung together can remind us that we are not in this alone; we are part of a community of faith.

God calls us to live in community. We are not solos; we are part of a choir—a congregation.

My earliest memory of "church" is of standing on a pew so I would be tall enough to share a hymnbook with my parents during the singing of congregational hymns in a Methodist Church in Bridgewater, Virginia. I was not even old enough to read the words in that mysterious, heavy, red-covered book of hymns, but I knew that it was the source of the wonderful, loving songs that were being sung by a church full of loving, caring people. In those songs and in the love of those people who sang them, God was present.

This memory reminds us why it is important to encourage children to be in worship with adults from a very young age. There is much in worship that they may not understand intellectually, but there is also much they can learn about *being* the church with others, and some of this learning happens through song.

When have the songs of the congregation been meaningful to you? Did you sing hymns on the day of a family member's baptism? When you gathered with other Christians for prayer on September 11, 2001? When you went with a handful of Christmas carolers to the homes of homebound church members? When you were on a mission trip and you had opportunities to sing with a congregation in another culture? Whether a thousand voices sing together in great harmony, or two or three gathered Christians sing the songs of faith they know by heart, Christ is in their midst, and God is glorified in the community of the church.

At their best, congregational songs are inspirational. "When a congregation sings together, the words of the hymn come alive to them and mean more than just a statement of fact. . . Worshipers experience the presence of God."[16] Hymns invite us and welcome us into a relationship with God.

> You give hymns and songs for singing, toes for tapping your good news,
> Organ sounding, hand bells ringing, faithful hearers in the pews.
> With the trumpet and the cymbal, with guitar and violin,
> Faith is found here and rekindled; hearts are lifted, once again.
> ("All The Music Sung and Played Here," third stanza)

Finally, we sing because our songs bring others into a closer relationship with God in Jesus Christ. Congregational singing is a way of reaching out to share God's joy with others. Because of this, the church needs to be willing to sing new songs that will speak to new Christians and to "seekers." There is beauty in many of the traditional hymn texts, but churches need to have an openness to singing new words on occasion.

One of the best comments I ever heard about one of my hymn texts was from a mother who reported on an after-church conversation she had had with her teenage son. After church one Sunday, he had told her, "I liked that middle hymn. I actually understood what the words meant."

Another person related the story about a time she was in church and the congregation sang a hymn that she hated. She shrugged her shoulders, and decided to sing it joyfully anyway. After worship the woman standing next to her said, "I was really feeling discouraged when I came to church. I'm dealing with a lot of personal problems. But when we started singing those hymns, and I heard you singing so joyfully next to me, you sounded like you really meant what you were singing. I started thinking about the words of that hymn, and it made me feel better." We sing not only for ourselves but out of love for others.

Once when I was leading a workshop on hymns, I asked the question: "What church song has special meaning in your life?" Some people answered by talking about beloved Christmas carols or songs they had learned years earlier at youth rallies. One woman came up to me after the program and told me a story. When her husband, a very dedicated Christian, was dying, she and her grown children had gathered around his bedside. Together they sang the hymns and songs of the church that had meant so much to all of them through the years. They sang for hours, sometimes singing from a hymnbook, sometimes remembering pieces of hymns from memory, until it was late and they were tired. One by one, they moved from singing to gentle, holy silence, until only the woman was singing to her husband. After a while she began to sing "What Wondrous Love Is This." She sang the whole hymn including these final words:

> "And when from death I'm free, I'll sing on, I'll sing on,
> And when from death I'm free, I'll sing on;
> And when from death I'm free, I'll sing and joyful be,
> And through eternity I'll sing on, I'll sing on,
> And through eternity I'll sing on."[17]

And as she sang those words, her husband died. She paused and told me that it was in that moment when she was singing that he became part of the Church Triumphant, and he began to sing praises to God for all eternity, just as the words of the hymn proclaimed.

We sing because God gives us the gift of song—to offer praise, to express our deepest prayers, to help us grow in our faith, to strengthen the church, and to share with others. Our songs may be imperfect now; some people cannot carry a tune. Others cannot hear, speak or understand, but they may be able to feel the rhythm of the music, or sign the words, or simply feel the presence of God's love as the congregation sings together. Sharing in the church's song is a Christian practice that prepares all God's people for an eternity of singing praises to God.

> Bless the talents we are bringing, for we offer you our best.
> If our gifts are not in singing, may our joyful noise be blest.
> If our world is ever silent, may we sign to you above.
> Touched by grace, may each one present offer back your song of love.
> ("All The Music Sung and Played Here," fourth stanza)

Notes

1. "Why We Sing" by Carolyn Winfrey Gillette was first printed in a 2006 issue of *Christian Reflections*, a journal of the Center for Christian Ethics at Baylor University. © 2006 The Center for Christian Ethics at Baylor University. All rights reserved. Used by Permission.

2. Brian Wren, *Praying Twice: The Music and Words of Congregational Song* (Louisville: Westminster John Knox Press, 2000), p. 84

3. Carolyn Winfrey Gillette, "All The Music Sung and Played Here," Copyright © 2000 Carolyn Winfrey Gillette.

4. Don Saliers and Emily Saliers, *A Song To Sing, A Life to Live: Reflections on Music as Spiritual Practice* (San Francisco: Jossey-Bass, 2005), p. 22.

5. Brian Wren, p. 87.

6. Don E. Saliers "Singing Our Lives" in *Practicing Our Faith: A Way of Life for a Searching People* edited by Dorothy C. Bass ((San Francisco: Jossey-Bass, 1997), p. 183.

7. Thomas G. Long, *Testimony: Talking Ourselves into Being Christian*, (San Francisco: Jossey-Bass, 2004), p. 47.

8. Ed Norman, "Music" in *The Complete Book of Everyday Christianity: An A-to-Z Guide to Following Christ in Every Aspect of Life* edited by Robert Banks and R. Paul Stevens (Downers Grove, IL: InterVarsity Press, 1997), p. 674.

9. Patrick Kavanaugh, *The Music of Angels: A Listener's Guide to Sacred Music from Chant to Christian Rock* (Chicago: Loyola Press, 1999), p. 7.

10. David Watson, *I Believe in the Church*, (London: Hodder and Stoughton,1982), p.192.

11. Quoted by John A. Huffman, Jr. in "Jesus Loves Me This I Know" (Christmas Eve sermon, December 24, 2003) available online at <http://www.standrewspres.org/sermons/serm122403.htm>.

12. Carolyn Winfrey Gillette, *Gifts of Love: New Hymns for Today's Worship* (Louisville: Geneva Press, 2000), No. 13.

13. Cesareo Gabarain, 1979 "Tu Has Venido a la Orilla/Lord, You Have Come to the Lakeshore" (translated by Gertrude Suppe, George Lockwood and Raquel Achon, 1988) *The Presbyterian Hymnal*, (Louisville: Westminster/John Knox Press, 1990), No. 377.

14. Elizabeth A. Johnson, "Mary, Mary, Quite Contrary," *U.S. Catholic*, December 2003, Volume 68; Number 12: pages 12-17, also available online at <http://www.uscatholic.org/2003/12/cov0312.htm>.

15. Patrick D. Miller, Jr., "In Praise and Thanksgiving," *Theology Today*, 1988, Vol. 45, No. 2, p. 180, also available online at <http://theologytoday.ptsem.edu/jul1988/v45-2-article3.htm>.

16. Brian Wren, p. 95.

17. American Folk Hymn, c. 1811 "What Wondrous Love Is This," *The Presbyterian Hymnal*, (Louisville: Westminster/John Knox Press, 1990), No. 85.

Indices
Biblical Index

Luke

Metrical Index

Topical Index

Aging and Gifts of Older Church Members

59. God, We Spend a Lifetime Growing

Anniversary, Church

20. Christ Taught Us of a Farmer
47. We Look to You, O Jesus
48. Looking Back, O God, We Wonder
49. God, We Join in Celebration
50. God, When You Called Our Church by Grace
51. When We Were a Younger Nation
53. God of Love, We Sing Your Glory
55. Lord, What a Cloud of Witnesses!

Ascension of the Lord

29. O Christ, When You Ascended

Baptism

12. Down by the Jordan
39. We Enter Your Church

Call/Vocation

 5. Our God, You Called to Moses
14. Jesus, You Once Called Disciples
15. O Lord, You Called Disciples
24. O Lord, As You Were On Your Way
39. We Enter Your Church
41. There Are Many Ways of Sharing

Disabilities Sunday

Easter

Eucharist/Lord's Supper

Evangelism

Families and Marriage

Funeral/Witness to the Resurrection

Grace of God

Holy Spirit

Jesus Christ, Ministry

Jesus Christ, Teachings

Justice

Sunday/Sabbath

Wealth and Possessions

Wholeness and Healing, Service of

Worship

Lectionary Index

Epiphany 5B
Isaiah 40:30-31   8. An Eagle Is Soaring

Epiphany 5C
Luke 5:1-11   15. O Lord, You Called Disciples

Epiphany 7A
Matthew 5:38-48   77. God, Whose Love Is Always Stronger

Epiphany 8A
Matthew 6:33   60. You Formed Us in Your Image, Lord

Epiphany 8C
1 Corinthians 15   30. Listen, Sisters! Listen, Brothers!

Epiphany 9A
Psalm 31:10   42. O God, We Rage at Hurtful Things

Epiphany 9B
Deuteronomy 5:15   36. O God, You Made the Sabbath Day

Epiphany 9C
Psalm 96   63. God, Bless the Poet's Heart and Hand

Transfiguration A
Matthew 17:1-13   24. O Lord, As You Were on Your Way
2 Peter 1:16-18   24. O Lord, As You Were on Your Way

Transfiguration B
Mark 9:2-13   24. O Lord, As You Were on Your Way
2 Peter 1:16-18   24. O Lord, As You Were on Your Way

Transfiguration C
Luke 9:28-36   24. O Lord, As You Were on Your Way

Ash Wednesday ABC
Psalm 51   7. O God, Be Merciful to Me

Passion C

Luke 22:14-19	10. Remember Me
Luke 22:14-23	6. Why Is This Night Different?
Luke 23:1-25	27. Our Lord, You Stood in Pilate's Hall

Maundy Thursday ABC

Exodus 12-13	6. Is This Night Different?
John 13:31-35	62. O God Our Creator, You Work Every Day
1 Corinthians 11:23-25	10. Remember Me
	40. We Come to This Table

Good Friday ABC

Psalm 22	37. All the Music Sung and Played Here
	42. O God, We Rage at Hurtful Things
John 18:28–19:6	27. Our Lord, You Stood in Pilate's Hall
John 19:25-27	14. Jesus, You Once Called Disciples
Hebrews 4:15	13. Our Lord, You Were Sent

Easter Vigil ABC

| Psalm 46:9 | 77. God, Whose Love Is Always Stronger |
| Romans 6:4-11 | 39. We Enter Your Church |

Easter C

| 1 Corinthians 15 | 30. Listen, Sisters! Listen, Brothers! |

Easter Evening A

| Luke 24:13-32 | 10. Remember Me |

Easter Evening B

| Luke 24:13-32 | 10. Remember Me |

Easter Evening C

| Luke 24:13-32 | 10. Remember Me |

Easter 2B

| 1 John 1:8 | 63. God, Bless the Poet's Heart and Hand |

Easter 2C

| Psalm 150 | 37. All the Music Sung and Played Here |

Easter 3A

Psalm 27:1
Luke 24:13-32

17. O God of Light, May Our Light Shine
10. Remember Me

Easter 3B

Luke 24:13-32
1 John 3:1

10. Remember Me
62. O God Our Creator, You Work Every Day

Easter 3C

John 21:1-14
Acts 9:1-22

28. Peter Said, I'm Going Fishing
14. Jesus, You Once Called Disciples

Easter 4A

Psalm 23
John 10:1-18
Acts 2:43-47

42. O God, We Rage at Hurtful Things
62. O God Our Creator, You Work Every Day
38. You Call Us, Lord, to Worship

Easter 4B

Psalm 23
Acts 4:11
1 John 3:18, 23

42. O God, We Rage at Hurtful Things
50. God, When You Called Our Church by Grace
35. Be Doers of the Word of God

Easter 4C

Psalm 23
Revelation 7:17

42. O God, We Rage at Hurtful Things
44. O God, Whose Loving Has No End

Easter 5A

Psalm 31:10
John 14:1-6

1 Peter 2:6

42. O God, We Rage at Hurtful Things
43. God, Your Love and Care Surround Us
44. O God, Whose Loving Has No End
50. God, When You Called Our Church by Grace

Easter 5B

Psalm 22

1 John 4:7,8
1 John 4:7, 8, 18
1 John 4:7-21

37. All the Music Sung and Played Here
42. O God, We Rage at Hurtful Things
68. Giving God, We Pause and Wonder
65. God, We've Known Such Grief and Anger
41. There Are Many Ways of Sharing

Trinity C

Psalm 8	1. The Earth Is the Lord's
Romans 5:8	62. O God Our Creator, You Work Every Day
Romans 5:8-10	9. We Love to Sound Your Praises

Proper 4A/Ordinary 9A

Psalm 46:9	77. God, Whose Love Is Always Stronger

Proper 4B/Ordinary 9B

Deuteronomy 5:15	36. O God, You Made the Sabbath Day

Proper 4C/Ordinary 9C

Psalm 96	63. God, Bless the Poet's Heart and Hand

Proper 5B/Ordinary 10B

Mark 3:20-35	60. You Formed Us in Your Image, Lord

Proper 6A/Ordinary 11A

Psalm 100	37. All the Music Sung and Played Here
Matthew 10:1-15	14. Jesus, You Once Called Disciples
Romans 5:8	62. O God Our Creator, You Work Every Day
Romans 5:8-10	9. We Love to Sound Your Praises

Proper 6B/Ordinary 11B

Mark 4:26-29	21. Christ, You Walked Among the Grain Fields
2 Corinthians 5:16-17	63. God, Bless the Poet's Heart and Hand
2 Corinthians 5:17	36. O God, You Made the Sabbath Day
	53. God of Love, We Sing Your Glory

Proper 6C/Ordinary 11C

Luke 8:1-3	14. Jesus, You Once Called Disciples
	15. O Lord, You Called Disciples
Galatians 2:17-21	31. For Freedom, Christ Has Set Us Free!

Proper 7A/Ordinary 12A

Matthew 10:1-41	14. Jesus, You Once Called Disciples
Romans 6:4-11	39. We Enter Your Church

Proper 7B/Ordinary 12B

Psalm 9:9   62. O God Our Creator, You Work Every Day

Job 38-39   63. God, Bless the Poet's Heart and Hand

Proper 7C/Ordinary 12C

Psalm 22   37. All the Music Sung and Played Here

     42. O God, We Rage at Hurtful Things

Galatians 3:26-27   60. You Formed Us in Your Image, Lord

Galatians 3:27   62. O God Our Creator, You Work Every Day

Galatians 3:27-28   31. For Freedom, Christ Has Set Us Free!

     33. No Longer

Proper 8A/Ordinary 13A

Psalm 13   66. God of Creation

Psalm 13:1-2   65. God, We've Known Such Grief and Anger

Matthew 10:1-41   14. Jesus, You Once Called Disciples

Proper 8B/Ordinary 13B

2 Corinthians 8:9   11. "Fear Not!" the Angel Said

Proper 8C/Ordinary 13C

Luke 9:58   62. O God Our Creator, You Work Every Day

Galatians 5:1, 19, 22-23   31. For Freedom, Christ Has Set Us Free!

Galatians 5:1   60. You Formed Us in Your Image, Lord

Galatians 5:14   19. Who Is My Neighbor?

Proper 9A/Ordinary 14A

Matthew 11:28-30   62. O God Our Creator, You Work Every Day

Proper 9B/Ordinary 14B

Mark 6:3   62. O God Our Creator, You Work Every Day

2 Corinthians 12:9   77. God, Whose Love Is Always Stronger

Proper 10A/Ordinary 15A

Psalm 119:105   17. O God of Light, May Our Light Shine

     63. God, Bless the Poet's Heart and Hand

Matthew 13:1-13   20. Christ Taught Us of a Farmer

Matthew 13:1-23   21. Christ, You Walked Among the Grain Fields

Proper 10B/Ordinary 15B

Psalm 24   1. The Earth Is the Lord's
Psalm 85:10   72. A Voice Was Heard in Ramah

Proper 10C/Ordinary 15C

Luke 10:25-37   19. Who Is My Neighbor?
                                 66. God of Creation

Proper 11A/Ordinary 16A

Romans 8:18-23   4. Creator God, You Made the Earth
Romans 8:22   77. God, Whose Love Is Always Stronger

Proper 11B/Ordinary 16B

Psalm 23   42. O God, We Rage at Hurtful Things
Mark 6:32-44   22. Where Is Bread?
                                 67. God, You Give Us Recreation

Proper 11C/Ordinary 16B

Luke 10:38-42   14. Jesus, You Once Called Disciples
Colossians 1:19   58. God, With Joy We Look Around Us
Colossians 1:20   70. God, How Can We Comprehend?

Proper 12A/Ordinary 17A

Matthew 13:33   49. God, We Join in Celebration
                                 74. Blest Are God's Peacemaking Ones
Romans 8:28-39   77. God, Whose Love Is Always Stronger

Proper 12B/Ordinary 17B

John 6:9   14. Jesus, You Once Called Disciples
John 6:1-15   22. Where Is Bread?

Proper 12C/Ordinary 17C

Psalm 85:10   72. A Voice Was Heard in Ramah

Proper 13A/Ordinary 18A

Matthew 14:13-21   22. Where Is Bread?

Proper 13B/Ordinary 18B

Psalm 51   7. O God, Be Merciful to Me

Proper 22C/Ordinary 27C

Psalm 137:1-2   73. Another Son Is Killed

Proper 23A/Ordinary 28A

Psalm 23   42. O God, We Rage at Hurtful Things
Philippians 4:4   9. We Love to Sound Your Praises

Proper 23B/Ordinary 28B

Psalm 22   37. All the Music Sung and Played Here
     42. O God, We Rage at Hurtful Things
Hebrews 4:15   13. Our Lord, You Were Sent

Proper 23C/Ordinary 28C

2 Timothy 3:15-16   63. God, Bless the Poet's Heart and Hand

Proper 24A/Ordinary 29A

Psalm 96   63. God, Bless the Poet's Heart and Hand

Proper 24B/Ordinary 29B

Psalm 104   2. On the Beach, the Waves of Waters
     3. Creator, We Thank You for All You Have Made
Job 38-39   63. God, Bless the Poet's Heart and Hand

Proper 24C/Ordinary 29C

Psalm 121:4   62. O God Our Creator, You Work Every Day
2 Timothy 3:15-16   63. God, Bless the Poet's Heart and Hand

Proper 25C/Ordinary 30C

Psalm 84:1,10   52. How Lovely Is Your Church, O Lord

Proper 26A/Ordinary 31A

1 Thessalonians 2:2   77. God, Whose Love Is Always Stronger

Proper 26B/Ordinary 31B

Deuteronomy 6:4-9   10. Remember Me

Proper 27A/Ordinary 32A

Amos 5:24   67. God, You Give Us Recreation
     71. God, May Your Justice Roll Down
Joshua 24:13   55. Lord, What a Cloud of Witnesses!

Proper 27B/Ordinary 32B

Proper 28C/Ordinary 33C

New Year ABC/Christ the King

Christ the King A

Christ the King B

Christ the King C

New Year ABC

January: Martin Luther King, Jr. Birthday

January: Week of Prayer for Christian Unity

Souper Bowl Sunday (First Sunday in February)

Earth Day Sunday (closest to April 22)

Mothers' Day/Christian Family Week

Memorial Day

Choir Dedication Sunday

September (First Sunday): Christian Vocation Sunday

World Communion Sunday

Thanksgiving A

Thanksgiving C

Title Index